DAREDEVIL TWILIGHT

Virginia Barton Brownback

Half Meadow Press
San Geronimo, CA
2003

Daredevil Twilight

All photographs by Virginia Barton Brownback

All maps, except where noted otherwise, by Mitra Van Vuren

Maps of Ukraine and Normandy by Susan Ishida

Book design and typesetting: Wordsworth, San Geronimo, CA

Printed in the United States of America on recycled paper

ISBN 0-9723269-2-8

"Rendezvous with the Old Men of Callanish" appeared in different form in *Modern Maturity*, December 1988.

"Blue Rinse in My Duffle" appeared in different form in *Nepal Traveller*, November 1987; *Los Angeles Times*, September 13, 1987; *Toronto Star*, January 30, 1988; *Ft. Worth Star-Telegram*, February 4, 1988; *San Francisco Chronicle*, March 6, 1988; *Denver Post*, September 25, 1988; *Montreal Gazette*, October 10, 1988; as "Euphoria in Nepal" in *India Currents*, November 1989; as "A Walk in the Annapurnas," in *Travelers' Tales Guides: Nepal*, 1997; and in *Travelers' Tales: A Mother's World*, 1988.

"Away from the Glitz" appeared in different form as "Heart of Kashmir," *Image Magazine*, March 19. 1989; as "Kashmir," in the *Los Angeles Times*, July 9, 1989; as "Backstage, Kashmir," in the *Ft. Worth Star-Telegram*, November 1989; as "Heart of Kashmir," in *India Currents*, May 1990; and in *Travelers' Tales: A Mother's World*, 1988.

"Slit in the Iron Curtain," appeared in different form as "Ukrainian Odyssey," in *Modern Maturity*, August 1989.

"Full Moon Over Rajasthan," appeared in different form in *India Currents*, February 1992; and the *San Francisco Chronicle*, August 1992.

"Lost Without Language" and "Divine Madness," appeared in different form as "Jumping Off," in *Modern Maturity*, August 1992.

"Tug of War Angkor," appeared in different form as "Temples of Chaos," *Modern Maturity*, February 1994.

"Voices from a Far Shore," appeared in different form in *Modern Maturity*, July 1994.

"The Unpaved Road," appeared in different form in *Modern Maturity*, May 1996; and *Travelers' Tales Guides: A Woman's Passion for Travel*, 1999.

Praise for *Daredevil Twilight* and Virginia Barton Brownback's storytelling:

"*Daredevil Twilight* pays tribute to the power of mature women to leave the boundaries of their homes and family, recreate themselves, push their limits, and find fulfillment through imaginative travel. She will inspire other women to put their fears on hold and just go! . . . What beautiful prose!"
— Marybeth Bond, Travel Expert, Author/Editor, *A Woman's World, Gutsy Women*

"In all the years I've taken the Los Angeles *Times*, I don't recall an article more enjoyable than the one on Nepal by Virginia Barton. How delightful! She's the kind of writer who might convince me to visit Southeast Asia during the Monsoon. Please — more of her adventures!"
— Nicky Kronick, San Diego

"You're a breath of fresh air. I read it laughing with pleasure. Please, I want more. We all need what you write about. Travel more, do books. And take me with you."
— Paula Mason, Beverly Hills, CA

"Dear Virginia, . . . just finished your article in *Modern Maturity* ("Jumping Off," 1993) and sat at the table looking out onto the patio for a long time afterwards, wonderful surges of enthusiasm racing through me . . . the knowledge that the only limitations in my life will be those that I choose. Thank you for affirming that life changes can be positive ones. Today is my 59th birthday. What a delightful gift your writing has given me!"
— Darlene Goutierez, Los Angeles, CA

"Virginia Brownback is the traveling companion you've been looking for all your life . . . She brings along a childlike delight in new vistas and a wisdom that makes the discoveries which are the real rewards of a long life."
— John Leggett, author/teacher:
"Ross and Tom," "A Daring Young Man"

"Evocative, lyrical in places, displaying courage and irrepressible inquisitiveness. Virginia's humanity, humor, powers of observation shine through . . . *Daredevil Twilight* is a model and an invitation to plunge into real, as distinct from canned, travel, for both sexes, and at any age."
— David Hooson, Professor Geography
University of California, Berkeley

"For twenty years or more I have watched Ginny Brownback leave and return from her 'compulsive explorations' of the forbidding corners of the planet. 'Who are you going with?' I would ask, in paternalistic horror at the idea of an 'older woman' traveling alone to Laos, Kashmir, the Outer Hebrides, and the Hindu Kush. 'No one,' she'd answer. 'Going alone,' a mix of pride and apprehension in her voice as she sped off. I now know that she was rarely alone. Here is the fine and challenging art of setting out to a place unknown and returning home with a blaze of wild memories, a deeper sense of how other worlds work, and a collection that will enchant the erstwhile traveler for decades to come."
— Mark Dowie, investigative historian

For
Brooke and Dorcy * Jesse and Sandy
And for Preb Stritter, who showed me how.

"All growth is a leap in the dark."

— Henry Miller

Table of Contents

III. Mavericks

IV. Three From Indochine

Coda

Prelude 1940 > 1950:

The Narrow Bed, Bryn Mawr, PA

Few of us can trace our basic inclinations as far as they began. Looking back to my own stifled adolescence, however, I find many signs that pointed to the future that evolved. For nearly a decade, beginning in my teens, I lived in a tiny world without doors. I had milliery tuberculosis (a blood-stream infection), at that time a disease without a cure. I was taken out of school. I had little mobility and no independence. In those days, the patient was ordered to drink milk, avoid any exertions, lie daily under an ultraviolet ray lamp and, if the germs spread to the lungs, move to a sanitarium and breathe in mountain air. Some got better. Many died.

I was not in pain, and I was surrounded by the best available professional care, plus an adoring, sensible and secure family. But I ultimately came to know that they could not protect me. My future had dropped away.

The illness fluttered to a halt when the "wonder drug" Streptomycin came on the market. I emerged at the end of the tunnel — alive, high — and close to fearless. I was 25 years old.

What others take for granted were, for me, deep satisfactions: marriage to my first love; the magical arrival of two children I'd been told I should never have; the education that began with the

9

Community College at 42 and has never stopped; and my last love, Mr. Travel.

Any glitches that followed my initiation under fire were a cinder in the eye to someone who had sat on the sidelines so long. Life didn't have to be perfect; I just wanted the chance to live it.

By the late 1970's, my role as "Domestic Engineer" was waning. As I passed my half-century and sadly separated from my husband of 24 years, travel became possible. Books and maps kept me up at night. The least accessible corners of the globe called the loudest. These places would teach me geography and history, snuff out provincialism and prejudices, show me what had been missing inside the parameters of my narrow bed.

I think of these as the twilight years. As my friends were welcoming grandchildren, joining AARP, and becoming firmly entrenched in their communities, I was shopping for suitcases and money belts. Once I took off, the inclinations of my daredevil twilight were to carve my own path and listen to my own voice.

It was the infinite variety of the human condition I was after. I had had enough of comfort and coddling: Gourmet presentations, serious shopping, the mint nestling in the satin of the turned-down bed in the 5-Star hotel — these were not why I longed for new vistas. I was stretching out for the life-giving jolts of culture shock.

I. First Stop, Europe

The road ahead (Hebrides).

"You went . . . . .alone?" my friends gasped.

"Couldn't you find . . . anyone . . . to go with you?"

I remember boarding my first international flight, stepping outside the airport terminal to the open runway, being hit in the face by a gust of raw wind and in the gut, by a jumping-off sensation. The couple ahead of me moved together up the rickety metal stairs. He carried both their heavy overcoats and the camera-bag, and she leaned into him as if she were on a ship at sea.

I was only me.

It did not fall over me for many moons that (most of the time) alone was going to be better.

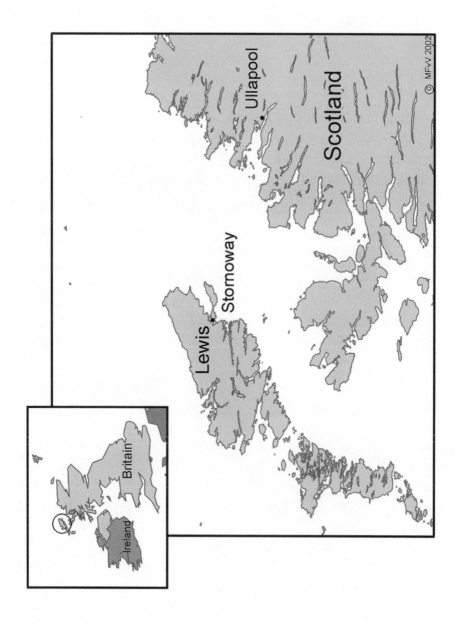

1   Rendezvous with the Old Men of Callanish:

Isle of Lewis, U.K.

One seems to stoop a bit, warming his hands in his pockets. One is a monk in a hooded cowl. Others wear capes that touch the ground and cluster around the 15 ½ foot-high altar stone. Together, leaning into the wind, they straggle across a bleak headland that overlooks East Loch Roag, a small bay opening out to the north Atlantic on the Coast of Lewis, the remotest of Scotland's Outer Hebrides.

These timeless sentinels are 48 pieces of the local Lewissean gneiss standing in the shape of a rough Celtic cross with some of the stones missing. I'd been in a hurry to get out to them, but I needn't have rushed. They've been there for at least 3,000 years.

Like all divine madness, my passion began in the imagination and pressed itself on me when I wasn't looking. Flipping through an out-of-date issue of *The National Geographic* encountered on a stranger's coffee table where one of my travel-mates took us for tea, I found myself drifting off from the conversation and flipping over and over to a double-page spread of stones in the moonlight. The site was almost off the map on a sheep and peat isle where Gaelic was the first language and the bloom of a daffodil in late June an event.

"One of Britain's most important prehistory circles," the caption read. But it wasn't the archaeology that particularly interested me. It was something less definable about the set of the stone shoulders thrust up against the clouds, huddled in that long conference. Locals, the article continued, call them the Old Men of Callanish. It fascinated me that they were uncut, but carefully selected stones.

"Someday . . . ." I thought to myself.

A couple of years later, in the muggy summer of 1978, when I was experimenting with my new single state and traveling nervously and a bit off-center after ending a 25-year marriage, a San Francisco friend who had swapped her flat for a row house outside of London, invited me to share it with her. Wonderful at first, the commute into the city became tedious, the lines at the Tower long and, after a while, I was gasping for fresh air and someplace else. Some place green, some uncrowded place with space.

"Aren't you going to Skye?" my friends inquired — the island that got rave notices.

"No!" I surprised myself by answering. "I'm going straight out to Lewis. I want to see the Callanish stones."

Next day I caught the 9:00 o'clock train to Glasgow, an all-day journey, and on the following day took a bus to Inverness, then another to Ullapool, the busy seaport that provides the most direct, northerly crossing to Lewis from the mainland. When I walked out onto the dock, hundreds of screeching gulls were circling the harbor trawlers and the 5:00 o'clock ferry was readying herself to take off in the pink twilight. As the ferrymen let the ropes go slack, my white hair and bifocals vanished, and I was that girl on another island singing, "I Know Where I'm Going."

On the open water the sea was black, the scones in the cafeteria damp, the coffee with steamed milk, warm and reassuring. Three hours out, Lewis loomed from a perpetual mist, treeless and unlovely — the whole island an unfinished sculpture of blue-gray metamorphic rock being slowly shaped by relentless winds.

We docked at Stornoway and I rang up the Mrs. MacLeod listed in my Bed and Breakfast guide. "Yes, m'love, I'm near the stones!" laughed the lady of the house.

Callanish turns out to be a village of about 40 houses and a post office. When our bus arrives the driver points to Number 33, a newish stucco box. The front yard's only adornment is a group of old tires piled in a neat circle and a mass of narcissus-like flowers under the parlor window.

The door is open. (No one locks their doors on Lewis, I am told; "No place for a thief to hide!") Mrs. MacLeod, in a tam-o'-shanter she seldom takes off, escorts me proudly to my freshly painted yellow room and recommends I sign up for her evening meal because "there's no place else to eat out." (She was right: there isn't.)

From my window I can see the stones whistling to me on the crest of a hill, a quarter-mile away.

I start out right away, past the pony in the field, past the red phone booth by the side of the road, past the "Antiquities" sign. Moving along a narrow tarmac lane and peering through a barbed-wire fence laced with sheeps' wool, I come closer and closer to the Old Men, inexplicably excited. Rain falls on my parka and the scene is colored gray.

It's quite a climb, and the stones are insignificant in the distance, dwarfed by the great wild landscape of their setting. I notice, as I gain height and perspective, that they are placed so they can be seen from a considerable distance, from several directions, and from out at sea; closer now, I have to admit, I am disappointed. Two Irish bikers have propped their handlebars against the waists of two stones and are using the stones as backrests while they munch sandwiches and drink sodas; it might be some Nordic playground!

Then, from the place on my map where it is marked True North, I start walking up "the avenue," pulled toward the tallest monolith, exactly as I had been pulled to the altar on my first visit to Westminster Abbey. It isn't easy, in either place, to stay on the periphery.

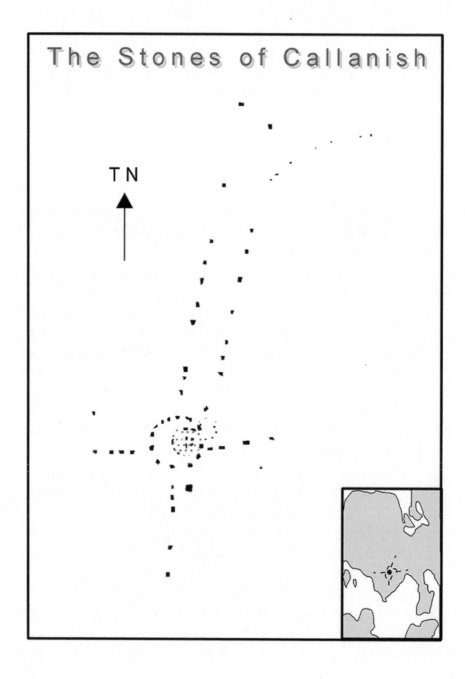

Suddenly the stones are towering over me. I have to stretch my neck to see the whole of the commanding guardians who form the central circle, all over eight feet tall, some as high as 12 feet. Here, I suppose, are the VIPs at the Speakers' Table, the High Priests, the High Court, the heroes. And here are the most human forms, with their hoods, capes and the attributes of men.

I know there are layers of history under the green at my feet. Seeing the grumpy northern light creep out for a moment to dance between clouds, land, water and the wrinkled stones, I let myself soak up the power that must have been in this place for early man.

The late American mythologist Joseph Campbell said living myth needs no explanation. When the riderless black horse in a military funeral passes, the boots turned backwards in the stirrups, words are superfluous. In this sense, myth is still alive at Callanish. Its remoteness, its climate, the poverty of the island allow the visitor a direct experience of the site — so unlike Stonehenge with its intrusive souvenir stands and fenced-off walkways, preventing the seeker from walking among the stones. Here, leaning back on a Bronze Age shoulder, I did not doubt I was in a rich and holy place.

Not all the visitors were so entranced. "Whatever do you suppose these people were thinking of?" a peevish Brit called out to the wind as he got off the tour bus for five minutes. He couldn't figure it out. Instant answers are missing.

Even when rigorous study is applied, answers are missing.

Archaeologists in general, proclaims Aubrey Burl ("Stone Circles of The British Isles," Yale, 1976) have been "taciturn about Callanish, seeing it as an enigma not easily solved by traditional methods." It's the astronomers, he adds, who have "welcomed the challenge of Callanish."

Gerald Hawkins sees it as a calendrical computer; Glyn E. Daniel as a "fusion of burial and ceremonial architecture." Prof. Alexander Thom, who first viewed the stones from a boat at sea and spent his professional life explaining them, sees Callanish as "a lunar site susceptible to the most refined observations." But

Burl contends that because Thom used "archaeologically out-moded" dates his hypotheses are a thousand years off.

Scholars keep pushing back the dates and now guess that the stones were erected between 2400 and 1350 B.C.E. The national Museum of Antiquities in Edinburgh exhibits beaker pots and axes from the area, and a visit there helps us visualize the Bronze Age farmers and hunters who were the architects of Callanish.

Back at Number 33, Mrs. MacLeod wants to make it clear that she herself sets no store by the stones. A strict Presbyterian, she is nonetheless too canny to discount entirely something that keeps her bedrooms full.

"Some people," she whispers, "think it hard to count the stones sometimes — always a different number. Others say that, if you visit them in the fog, you're sure to see them moving around!"

Of course, she doesn't believe any of it.

Mrs. MacLeod is incensed that the resident researcher, Margaret Ponting, is "making money off the stones" by selling her books — as if she, an outsider from Ipswich, knows anything special about their stones.

The next morning at the site, I chat with a woman passing on her way to market. Her eyes roll when I tell her I have come a long way — from California — to see her stones. I'm not sure she believes me.

"What do you think of them?" I ask her.

"Aye, nothin' at all!" she answers briskly. "They were here before we were born, and they'll be here when we're gone."

I stay ten days on this quiet island that progress has been slow to reach. One bus in the early morning runs the 50 kilometers to the north end, and returns as the afternoon wanes, to gather up the school children. After hours of waiting on wind-swept corners, I rent a car. With wheels of my own, I find long white beaches on the east side, a blackhouse at Arnol, an abandoned crofting village on a cove near Garynahine and a 30-foot-tall broch (double-walled circular stone tower), built to ward off Roman invaders at Dun Carloway.

The Callanish stones, Isle of Lewis, Hebrides.

Resident B.& B. hosts turn their living rooms over to me and share their best porcelain. When my rental car breaks down, neighborhood men push it to a garage, and the man who works on it all afternoon refuses to accept any money. ("I didn't fix it!" he says.) When my cold sounds like its moving towards bronchitis, Mrs. MacLeod hovers over me with a mustard plaster, murmuring. "You're so brave to travel alone!"

Mrs. MacLeod has never been off the island, though she had thought of going once or twice. At her table I hear how to dip a sheep and salt a mackerel. The heart of her house is the telephone outside my bedroom, where she chats with her close-ones, in both English and Gaelic, and I learn something about talk as play.

My trysting hour with the Old Men is after the evening meal. That's when sheep run along the great avenues chased by their keepers, and boys play Hide and Seek in the long dusk that lingers till midnight. I sit at the feet of the stones, sinking my spine into the tall support of my favorite's Renaissance cape and run my fingers along its cold folds.

Often I wonder who else has rested here. Who was it that first chose this slab as mentor? Who moved him from the ridge a mile to the northeast, where local legend says these raw stones first resided. Sometimes, trying to test the astronomers' theories, I position myself between a pair of stones, wondering if they could have predicted the shortest day of the winter solstice and the turning of the light — or the moment of an eclipse. How I wish the mute stones could describe some of the ceremonies they presided over, or sing me some of the music they have heard.

But — for this traveler, at least — the stones need never be decoded. Much of their charm, like that of all seasoned fascinators, is that though the Old Men of Callanish may whisper something new in my ear each time I visit them, they are, ultimately, unknowable. I have found a place that reaches further back in time than I can imagine, where the hands of the builders are still warm on their artless work of art.

2   Lost without Language:

Rome

It was four years before I jumped off again, this time to Milano, where my suitcase comes down the baggage ramp tied up with rope, and I can't find *aiuto*! (help!) in the Berlitz book. Italians aren't living up to their warm, cuddly image either. Men don't pinch, like we've all heard, but on my first outing to the outdoor opera, push me unceremoniously aside, to get ahead in the espresso line. I am instantly disenchanted, suspecting I have arrived in a place where a woman alone spells "opportunity."

An acquaintance has lent me her car in which I drive from Firenze to Siena, a walled city with four or five gates, footpaths at its core and a number of one-way streets with no exits.

On my first evening, it takes me a long time to find my way out of the maze of streets. As night falls and I become frustrated and famished, I stop searching for a picture out of Gourmet magazine and sit down in a drab place where I am the only customer. The waiter, an adorable, callow youth, helps me order the only items I can read on the menu: pasta with *carne* sauce, *fromage* and *vino blanco*.

After I finish and pay my bill, I ask for directions back to my country *pensione*. Unable to make my waiter understand, I lead him to the road signs out in front and ask him — in no language he has ever heard — to point to which road I should go back on. Next thing I know, he is leading me — gently — off in another direction, not to the restaurant, not to an intersection, but into the bushes behind the restaurant, with something else in mind, which I am slow to comprehend.

When I "get the message," I am so startled that the few Italian words I have memorized evaporate.

"No! No!" I respond mechanically. Then — insanely — I start repeating "*Su madre! Su madre!*" What I mean is: "I am old enough to be your mother, whatever are you thinking?" But I don't have the words.

The young man understands the body language, backs away instantly — blushing — repeating, "I'm sorry, I'm sorry!"

Ultimately, I am the one feeling ashamed to be caught as the aging innocent, blundering through his country bereft of language.

A few days later, I do the unthinkable: I drive south on the *Autostrada* to Rome, now in a rental car. Ferraris pull into the outside lane, lean on the horn and pass me, flying. By the time I get to the toll gate into the Holy City, I am unnerved in a sudden downpour. I can't find the switch to turn on the windshield wiper and am driving blind. So I pull over into a Bus Stop, lean out the window, and ask a woman standing there the way to the Eden hotel, where I have made a reservation.

"I'll show you," she says, hopping into the passenger seat next to me before I can protest. "I live nearby."

At this point I need a person who speaks English like a desert wanderer needs water; maybe this is my lucky day, I think. But "near" turns out to be a long joyride to HER front door, while she chatters in Italian and I respond in English.

I don't get much of it. She keeps repeating: "*Papa morte! Papa morte!*"

"Your father is dead?" " I answer her. That's what it sounds like.

Twenty minutes later, at the front door to her apartment, she waves me vaguely on in the direction of my hotel. I stop several times to make further inquiries. When, at last, I get there and settle in, all the talk on the roof garden is about the world leaders who will be arriving for the funeral of Pope Paul VI, which will take place tomorrow.

I have landed in Rome on August 11, 1978. Under the spectacular, baroque *baldachin* of St. Peter's, with the Swiss guards holding their spears upright at the four corners, the body of the Pope — 'Papa' in Italian — is lying in state. That's the momentous news of the day that my hitchhiker was reciting, crying out the headlines, like a street-corner paperboy: "The Pope is dead!" "The Pope is dead!"

He has been lying in state for two days. Now, at five o'clock, there is to be a service at St. Peter's. My first thought is to go, but at the hotel, the desk clerks are horrified at the idea.

"Expecting five thousand!" they tell me. "A pickpocket's dream! You won't see anything without a reserved seat, and these are only for the VIP's. Much better to watch here from the hotel, on TV." What lunacy! I didn't land here at this propitious moment to watch on TV.

So I put on my black skirt, leave most of my money behind, get in a taxi at 4:20. When I tell the taxi driver "*St. Pietro*," he gives me a skeptical look, but pushes forward into the increasingly dense traffic. When the car comes to a standstill, I get out and go on by foot. Suddenly, I am on the edge of the Grande Piazza, which at this rare moment, is coming alive to enfold the thousands for whom it was designed.

I inch ahead over the cobblestones, but soon find myself blocked, not only by people, but by a TV truck. The cathedral is within sight, and I don't think I can get much closer. What I need is a little height. The truck has a running board. I climb up and find something to hang on to. From here I have a clear view of the raised stage and decide to stick with this perch, for now. The service has begun; I'm not sure what's happening, but the music swelling out through the loudspeakers is heavenly.

When I hear a voice close to me, on my right, whisper, "Amazing!" I jump at the English, turning in a flash to find, on the bumper next to me, the interpreter I had longed for: someone who knows both languages and something about the Pope and Rome.

Tony turns out to be an Australian journalist, stationed in the city. He tells me that this Pope has incurred enemies by trying to take away some of the privileges of the aristocracy, that he tried to be a People's Pope. He stipulated that he wanted an outdoor mass so that it would be accessible to all, that he should have the simplest cypress casket, with no adornments on stage except the one massive, tall candle — standing for Eternal Life.

It was a two-hour ceremony with the visiting Kings, Prime Ministers, Presidents, Ambassadors, Heads of State seated, while the hierarchy of the Catholic church moved through its ancient rituals. The bishops were elegant in their colorful mitre/head-dresses and vestments, glistening with gold thread, chanting in Latin, walking slowly back and forth from the makeshift altar at stage-center-back, carrying prayer-books and huge silver chalices. Towards the end of the service, 50 priests in simple black cassocks with white aprons over them, came down the steps into the plaza, carrying the great chalices, the bread and wine, as they moved through the crowd, offering the sacrament of Holy Communion to anyone in the audience who wanted it.

While this was happening, the sun began to set, and the air cooled down. All around, the crowd, in its best clothes and on its best behavior, murmured to each other and to their children, instructing them. It seemed to me the safest corner of the world I could be in at that moment.

As the high priests swung the incense lantern up and around and over the coffin, the sun disappeared behind the two enormous arms of the colonnades that enwrap the mammoth piazza. Pink floodlights came on and played on the statues of St. Peter and St. Paul, which dominate the square. The birds sprang to life and swallows swooped around the bell tower and over our heads as they rang the glorious bell and the celebratory voices sang out, in the language of every nation where the Catholic church is dominant.

The undertakers laboriously carried the coffin shoulder-high, down the great steps towards the crowd in the square, an unmistakable gesture of display, I thought. Everyone who had come — the people — must have a chance to pay their Papa homage. When he had been seen by all, they slowly turned in a wide circle, before lifting him once again up the stairs and through the massive doors of the *Bascillica*, for the burial. At the turn of the closing circle, as the entourage gradually began to disappear into the cathedral, the clapping of hands began. Soon, every Italian in the square, and every visitor, was clapping — to say "good-bye!" — and with the clapping, they shouted over and over *"Papa morte! Papa morte!"*

As I tell this story, 20 years have gone by, but the shapes and sounds, even the smells are all retrievable: the wine, the incense, the women's perfume — the swallows' wing-tips blowing wind in my ear.

The event was honorific on an almost unimaginable scale, but personal as well. A man was there, as well as a Pope. In the forms of the liturgy and music by which the centuries-old Roman Church responds to the end of the journey — whose ever it might be, king or clod — the meanings were universal, unmistakable in any language. For once, I didn't need the Berlitz book.

I have never been tempted to return to Rome, to try to recapture the butterfly elements of that first synchronistic connection of time — place — and the lucky wanderer.

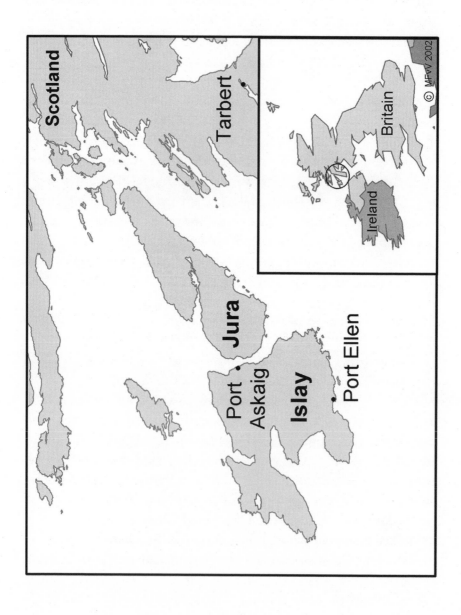

3   Divine Madness:

Isle of Islay, U.K.

It's the island that goes away,
not we who leave it.

— Ian Crichton Smith

I was still in the amateur archeologist phase of my early travels, following in the footsteps of a team named Colin and Janet Bord in search of the more striking stones scattered over the Dartmoor and Cornwall. After taking to the north seas to find the wonderful Callanish "men" in the Outer Hebrides, I got hold of Jemima Tindall's *Scottish Island Hopping,* a treasure full of contour maps and details about each and every one of the Shetland, Orkney, Hebridian, Clyde, and Forth islands. For a while, I thought I might be spending every summer for the rest of my life ferrying, biking, chasing after the antiquities hidden in the brambles of the Western Isles.

This summer I was on the way to the remote island of Jura where deer were said to swim in the sea. My archeology books described its two spectacular hills with a steep valley dividing them as "the Paps of Jura." These mounds were thought to be crucial sighting marks used by early man on Scotland's Kintyre peninsula, to trace the year-round path of the sun and moon as they rose and fell between the clefts of the two rounded ridges.

The only ferry to Jura came from Port Askaig, Islay (pronounced "eye-lah"), a ten-minute crossing; I would just slip over to Islay for a night before continuing on. I had a small backpack, good boots, a camera, a journal, no fixed itinerary, and all the time in the world. I did not realize that fate was preparing a detour for me on that stepping stone.

Following the same scenic route along the green highland country as the summer before, I crossed on the car-ferry from the tip of Kintyre peninsula to Islay's biggest town, Port Ellen. There, seeing no inviting B & B's, I took a room at the modest White Hart Hotel. Dropping off my bag, weary, and hoping for a warming drink and a quick supper, I stumbled into what I thought to be the hotel lounge and bar, only to find myself in a drab and darkish place.

"Doesn't look as if I've chosen much of a hotel," I said to myself. In fact, I was no longer in the tourist hotel, but in "the public bar" — the classic village pub, headquarters for news and gossip, where the men of the village came to have a beer or a couple of shots of whiskey at the end of the day.

Bone cold, by then — and confused about where I was — I sat down at a tiny table and timidly asked for a wee dram of the local brew "with ice!"

"Oh! A Yankee bird!" the bartender teased, whereupon the attendant eavesdroppers roared. There were only a few locals sitting around and I was evidently on display.

At my table, I spread out the map I had brought, contemplating the next day's walk. "Might as well see what's here," I thought. When the waitress came with my drink, I pointed to a mark on it and asked: "How far is it to your Standing Stone?"

From a corner, far left, a somewhat damaged Norse God rose and moved towards us. He was sporting a blond/gray beard and wearing a tired, greenish tweed suit — not entirely clean — and rubber boots. He shooed the girl away with a hand and a grumble.

"She doesn't know anything," he said, taking over. He took a seat next to me, bringing along his glass of stout. As soon as he opened his mouth, I knew he was no typical peat-digger. The voice was Richard Harris in Camelot.

"We don't have any important monoliths," he said. "But it was from here that the Lord of the Isles ruled Scotland, as far back as 1156. There's a castle, though there's not much of it left."

My knowledge of Scottish history was dim, but this man knew it all and, I was soon to discover, a fierce Scot's nationalistic; he didn't, for one minute, want to be "British." I told him my name and asked his.

"Sean Patrick Michael Kevin Macdonald O'Leary," he recited — fast.

"Really?" I asked. I thought it was a joke.

"I was born in Scotland, but I had an Irish mother," he laughed. "I'm an artist," he added, which I doubted also. But it was a pretty good line; he had my full attention.

Gradually his friends wandered over: Bertie, the 70-ish widower, effusively winning, Declan, 32, darkly handsome, devilish, who worked in the distillery married to an Australian and seemed to be the son Sean had never had. We all ended up sitting together at a bigger table, and they made a great fuss over Sean and over me. I was the new "lassie," and it was understood that their elderly ringleader had moved in first. In an hour I learned more about island life than a tourist on the other side, in the spiffed-up White Hart lounge, would have learned in a month.

Islay is a piece of undeveloped real estate 30 miles long, never more than 15 miles across, where "a sunny day" means it isn't raining. Famous for the single-malt Scotch whiskey it brews from its peat soil, it looks out, from its wildest northwest corner, towards Ireland.

I wasn't planning to make a full-stop here, but I found myself slowing down. These characters said they would be waiting for me, the following night, in the same place.

The next day I went out alone on the walk I had planned, got as far as I could on foot. I found a monolith and took its picture, but it was many long miles between the "sites." By afternoon, my feet hurt and I found myself looking forward to that "pick me up" later in the bar. This time I entered brazenly from the street door.

At first, I didn't recognize anyone. Then my new comrades dribbled in about sunset, and it was the same as before: The charm was in the talk — the way they did it. And I couldn't seem to stop laughing. "Working-class blokes" would be how they saw themselves, I suppose, but none of them fit neatly into my categories. I was stumped by their lyrical speech and wild humor, accepting life as it came to them, which — coupled with their facile grasp of history and literature — made me think they were highly "educated." Yet their lack of ambition and their lifestyle didn't jibe. They lived in temporary rooms and in trailers; they worked at odd jobs when there was work and bartered the rest of the time. They alluded good-naturedly to seedy patches in their past, but I couldn't call them "tough"; all ages, they were a bunch of rowdy lads, romping through the heather.

Emphatic about everything, they insisted I needed a car. The best places which I HAD to see, were "far away" (over five kilometers). Sean offered to show me his island, if I could get a vehicle. I was determined to go. Angus, who ran the garage up the street, might have something he would loan me for the day.

Sean agreed to meet me next morning at the entryway to the White Hart. It was sunny and windy, and I had maps. He was there ahead of me and seemed nervous. In the glare, he looked older than he had in the pub.

I drove, left side, and we circumnavigated the island, stopping frequently, walking up to the 900 BCE Celtic cross, and finding another stone circle, with the monoliths long ago fallen. Otherwise the island revealed thousands of sheep, secluded beaches with dune grasses and a dearth of people.

As we rounded the corners of Islay, stopping at favorite coves and hangouts, talking, talking, talking, a life unfurled. Sean had been to school in England; he's been a sailor and in the Naval Signal Corps during the war — married once, briefly, wife killed in the London blitz. His murals were on the walls of two of the local pubs, depictions of the townspeople cavorting along the walls — inventive, amusing, painterly. He had a gift for portraiture; there was a photography book about his work that I saw later, *The Island Artist*. But all this was some time ago. He was having trouble painting now — his eyes, he said.

We progressed from flirtatious talk to a hesitant kiss in what was left of the castle ruin. There was nothing imagined about the feelings. I hoped I knew how he felt, but I *knew* how I felt.

He was arrogant and shy, inept and bright, intense, funny and, like his island, full of music. I'd never known anyone who had so little and was so elegant. Everything he said and did was unexpected.

"What would it be like," I asked myself, "to live on this island?"

That evening, after our car-tour, he had promised Declan to baby-sit their toddler, so I dropped him off and had dinner alone at the White Hart, where I decided during the long hour of the leisurely meal, that it was time to leave.

I was just trying on someone else's life, I suspected. Already wandering outside familiar boundaries, where no "Permission Slips" were necessary, it was tempting to turn off on a different bend in the road, the obvious next step for someone who aspires to be "at home in the world" — maybe the only real adventure left in so-called Adventure Travel.

Sean knew I was hoping to get over to Jura; I told him that the first night. "You won't get anywhere on your own," he'd answered. "There's only one dirt-track down the middle of the island, take you hours on foot or by bike. But I could take you, have some wonderful friends who live there. You'd be dotty for each other. He's a history buff . They would put us up and take us around."

I had been tempted, but now I was talking myself out of it. I was too old to lose my heart in the Hebrides. I must move on —

tomorrow — as I had intended all along. Jura would have to wait. I left a "good-bye" note at the pub for Sean and returned to my room to reorganize my pack for the next lap.

When I got on the ferry to the mainland next day, resigned to departure, leaning on the rail, my nose deep in my guide book, with visions of Mull's "soft beauty" in my head, I had a breathtaking surprise.

Two strong arms grabbed me from behind in a vigorous hug and there the man was, laughing at me from behind his shaggy beard. I couldn't quite believe the sight of him!

"I thought you never left the island!" I said.

"I'll just come along with you to the next town up the line, Tarbert."

"You mean really have some time together?"

"Why not?" he yelped like a young puppy, picking me up off the ground and twirling me around a couple of turns.

Who was this wild man, willing to seize the day with no holds barred? How refreshing compared to the offshoots of uptight Puritan stock I had known most of my life! Had this ever happened to me before, wife of 25 years, mother of two? If it had, it was so far back, the memory was a smudge-pot.

My cheeks were burning, my heart racing. I knew I was grinning like an idiot. I was in for it. The Greeks, I had been told, had a name for this; they called it "the divine madness."

But this was to be no seamless plot. Within minutes, my new fellow was gesturing in the direction of a smiling, ruddy-faced man in a kilt and his round, hearty Scottish wife, crying, "Oh my God, Billy and Mavis!" We tried to disappear, but they had seen us. They lived on Islay; he had a business in London. They were utterly superfluous to our plans. We had to be nice all the way over, as they tried to include us in their plans and we tried to think how to fade into the distance without being rude.

The Scots are, in general, a conventional people and the islands exist in a time warp; Mr. and Mrs. Kilt did not sing along with women's lib or even with Cole Porter's "crazy flings." Sean tried to laugh off the situation, but their appearance was a snag in our impetuous getaway. They wanted us to join them for supper, and we made up lies — errands in Tarbert — a car on the other side. What evolved was an interminable summer evening in a busy port town on Saturday night, in which the impossible dreamers couldn't find a love-nest.

Our idyll spoiled, when we did find a room, we slept little and managed next morning (not giving clocks and schedules our full attention) to miss both Sean's ferry back to Islay and mine onwards. I felt star-crossed as I finally got underway and, when it started to rain, the weather matched my depressed mood.

The following weekend after saying I wouldn't, I came back to Islay to go with Sean to Jura.

While I was gone, I made one phone call back to the island from one of those booths covered with branches in the woods on the mainland. By now, I was a wavering puppet on a string. I had just about decided to give in, but before I took another detour, I wanted to make sure this erratic man still wanted to go on this excursion. After the usual struggle dialing in the dark and counting the change, I got through to him on the pub phone. Out of the damp-dark where I was huddled in my windbreaker asking the questions, his voice, like-no-other, came directly into my ear: "Aye, of course! of course! Are ya daft?? — I love you!"

I realize now this divine madness was always about his talking — in a language I knew but had never HEARD before. Not innately a good listener, all of a sudden, I was straining to listen to every word, leaning closer, sitting on the edge of my seat. It wasn't that he said anything brilliant, but that he introduced me to an exuberance of expression and passion, on almost any subject, such as I had never encountered — all combined with a lyrical imagination. He was a storyteller of the first rank.

I couldn't have lived with him a week, but I was in such a tear to get back after that provocative phone call that, like an irresponsible teenager, I blew the tired tire of my rental car, hurrying too fast over the winding roads.

When the weekend came, and we finally managed to cross over to stay with his oldest friends, the MacKenzie Sproats, those two days on Jura were as good as it got.

About 300 souls lived on the remote island in 1978, and our hosts were embedded in the community. MacKenzie Sproat published the only newspaper on the island, a monthly. Typeset by hand, printed using a combination of a hand litho and a 100-year-old treadle machine, it told of storms damaging Duncan Buie's lobster boat and plans to increase the economy by installing a knitwear factory. His wife was THE teacher responsible for the one-room Small Isle School, which went up to the 8th grade. The deer-island is also known for its ocean birds which Mac Sproat resembled. Ex-sailor and wireless operator, he was a light, upbeat, quick-moving man, who swooped around like one of the gannets in the books of illustrated local poetry he was proud of getting into print.

The Sproats had known Sean well for many years; they seemed genuinely fond of each other. I could see him, through their eyes — when he was in his prime and had his life before him. I could see what had been there. We spent the night in their simple, newish, bright house; they dropped everything to take care of us and show us "the old things." All the next day, we moved laboriously around the island in an old car that Mac had to start each time with a coathanger.

The cemetery was haunting. Everyone who had come before to the island was captured in the place, each stone unique, with here and there a cluster of the yellow gorse thrown over them. Mac translated the Gaelic poems carved into the stones and told us many an island yarn. It was the best introduction we could had to the place, or, in fact, to each other.

I still have a picture Mac took of me that day with my impossible lover, leaning against a hand-hewn rock wall on Jura — leaning against each other — with the horizon and the sea visible over our shoulders. He's smoking a pipe. I look skinnier than I ever believed I was — and we look so happy — almost as if we both belonged there.

After our return to Islay there was another interlude in a handsome driftwood house, sitting by itself out on a high moor, where Declan and his family were temporarily staying. His wife, who yearned for her home in Australia, was drawn to outsiders and asked us over for lunch. We munched on rough hunks of cheese and homemade bread in their kitchen, took a long, restless walk over headland pastures, backtracking on the same roads, over and over. As on all the other islands, friends were the source of most pleasures.

But it was beginning — all of it — to have the feel of aftermath. Each reencounter was a little less perfect.

At the end — naturally — we had a huge row — no doubt the only way to wrench ourselves away. It was easy to argue. We were two strong people, operating on a different grid. He had no clues for interpreting an independent American woman; and I had no clues for deciphering a proud Scot/Irish man, stranded on an impoverished island.

On a foul, gray day, when not one good thing happened, I took the last ferry out. He mumbled about making the trip over with me, but in the end, he stood firm on the dock of his island — a solid, immobile statue wrapped in yellow foul-weather gear, until, as the stretch of water increased between us, he shrank to the smallest, golden speck. I had my eyes fastened on his, even after I couldn't quite see them.

When I wrote, from the mainland — from harbors down the line — and then , more urgently, as I wended my way back to California — there was only silence. He knew ours was not a moveable feast; we had no other place to go.

Now, more years gone by than I like to think about, I remember the sounds. Of Gaelic. Of the screeching gulls and the fierce sea breezes. Of his voice raised in playful bombast — the mix of humor and poetry.

On one of our best nights — near the beginning — his voice, a low murmur close to my ear, tells me a secret:

"The Celts," he says, "live in two worlds."

For a brief time, I had tried.

II. Farther Afield

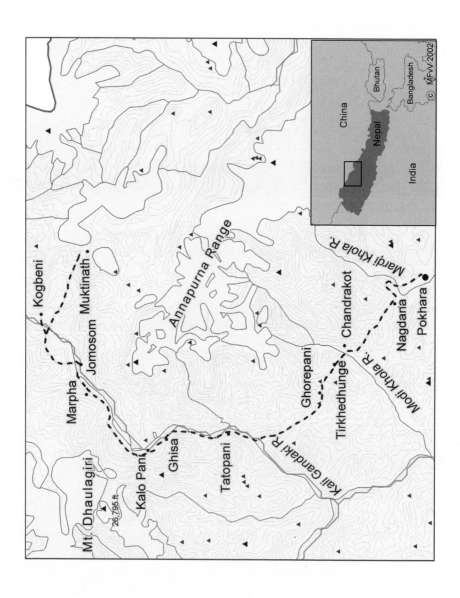

4   Blue Rinse in My Duffle:

Teahouse Trekking, Nepal

On a steep rise near Lumle a Nepali woman passes me, a *doko* basket with twigs straining against her forehead. She reaches out, grabs my hands in hers, and cries, "*Namaste!* Mother!"

My Nepali sister prays that I will make it up the hill. Dismayed, I suck in my stomach and try to look strong. Soon I realize that, at 62, I am a novelty traveling up the Kali Gandaki River gorge with my banner of white hair.

Some quick research on my fellow travelers — the Western ones — leads me to discover that they're from every country, with an age range from 18 to 30. Half are on their college break, while the other half have just ditched their first careers to reappraise their futures in an affordable Third World place. I am the only one with blue rinse in my duffle.

If this had been the route to the Everest Base Camp, a dearth of senior citizens would have been no surprise, but this is a moderate trek, mostly under 10,000 feet — hardly a thin-air ordeal. It's about 60 miles from Pokhara to Jomson, another 15 to the outpost town of Kogbeni (9,200 feet) and eastwards up to Muktinauth at 12,475 feet. My plan is to go as far as I can but I have serious doubts about that last, steep climb. At

41

Man cradling baby, near Chandrakot, Annapurna trail, Nepal.

Jomsom, I know there's an airstrip and a choice of flying out instead of returning by the same route.

The Pokhara-Jomsom trail follows an ancient trade route where there have always been inns for the traveler in almost every town. Reservations, unless you're with a group, are unnecessary; so is hauling in a tent, a camp stove, or dehydrated noodles. This trail is in fact the classic choice for what has come to be called "teahouse trekking," or — sometimes — "soft trekking." It is also known for the spectacular variety of its people and its landscape. Anyone who enjoys walking a few miles a day can do it — anyone, that is, who is willing to accept the sudden turn of the weather in the mountains and the jolt of another culture. Crucial for wimps and the unconditioned, however, is the porter system.

Let's face it: plenty of people, at any age, never consider the idea of trekking because the sight of a backpack gives them a headache. They don't want to carry an ounce, the body being enough of a cumbersome burden, especially climbing uphill. The porter system solves all that. In Kathmandu and Pokhara, and in most entryway villages into the mountains in Nepal, crowds of young men and women fight to be the one to carry your load. At first I worry about exploiting them; paying for their food and about $5 a day for their labor doesn't seem fair. But I come to feel guilty because I can use only one at a time. They depend on tourists to drive their economy.

My first porter, Purna, 28 and a married man, finds me at Lake Phewa in Pokhara. I am lounging by the lake in a three-room place where he comes around daily to offer his boat for rent by the hour. He takes me across to get a better look at the fabulous "Fish-Tail" mountain swishing its white peaks into the clouds.

"Don't you want to go trekking?" he asks. "I know all the trails."

He carries a tattered notebook with him, full of reports from satisfied customers. What impresses me is his fluent English and the story he tells about acquiring it.

Some years ago, he said, he was acting as a private guide for a man from Holland who fell and broke his leg two days out on the trail. Somehow, Purna managed to get him back and stayed with him, nursing him until the patient was well enough to fly. To show his gratitude, the Dutchman took Purna home with him, where for several months, he saw Europe and learned English. Purna showed me a scrapbook of these adventures in the west.

Although Purna and I started off well, it turned out to be the wrong time for him to be traveling. All of Nepal would soon be celebrating the greatest family celebration of the year — Desain. I asked him if this might be a problem before we made our plans, but he waved aside my concerns.

"Oh no! That won't matter," he cried. "I will bring my wife home material for a new sari, and she will be happy!"

But it wasn't that simple. Five days from his lake was like five years to him. When he began to cough loudly as we plowed through the rain into an inn at Ghorapani, complaining that my light pack was heavy, I knew he wanted to go home.

Around the fire that evening, I confided to a bilingual agricultural advisor, there from London, working in the area. "Hire another porter!" he suggested, as if this would be a cinch. In fact, it was.

In no time, he found Ram Chandra, 21 and unattached, dying to venture farther north and practice his English. The only serious problem that developed was that the shorts and sandals he had on were the only clothes he had with him, which I didn't know until we reached 9,000 feet and goosebumps appeared on his legs.

To both men, soft foothills Hindus of the Chetri caste (neither of whom turned out to be fully prepared for the high country) I was Mother, an antique of uncertain durability who must be protected. Purna liked to walk ahead and call back, "Watch out for that loose stone!" and Ram got me over the trembling log bridges by pulling me across with both hands, walking backwards while I walked forward. When they needed money, they came to me (I bought the long pants), and when I needed muscle, I went to them. When we had simultaneous blisters, we split the moleskin.

For me, the essential issue was to set my own pace. I knew I wanted to walk, at most, five or six hours a day. I wanted to browse. "No problem!" said Purna — until, out on the trail, his patience was tried as he waited for me to record flute music, watch millet being ground by a foot-hammer or photograph the work-dance of men twisting dried grass into skeins — all to him, the dull occurrences of daily life.

Along this major path between Nepal and Tibet, both men and animals have been moving goods since ancient times. Salt and wool came south; rice, sugar and kerosene, north. The traveler today still spends a lot of time leaping sideways as he hears the warning donkey bells, then watches the decorative plumes of red-dyed horsehair bob past. Animals in upper-crust pack trains wear Tibetan carpet bridles over their noses and blankets you would proudly hang on the wall. Other beastly hazards we encountered were the sleek, black water buffalo, who, it is rumored, enjoy lunging at tourists. (They can spot them.) Hordes of skittish goats, their silky, long hair brushed with fuchsia and ochre markings, traffic-jammed the trail more than once.

By the side of the trail, hair is cut, teeth are pulled, people sleep, cook, visit, work, and pass the news. On their way to school, two sisters climb a while with me up a winding stone staircase. "One, two, three, four, five — rest — pant!" I repeat as we ascend together. They giggle hysterically, and memorize my strange words in minutes.

An old, toothless man, barefoot, with the legs of a runner, shoots past me unwinded, toting a bulky, lopsided bundle. At the top of the ridge, where I stop to gasp audibly, he looks at me in my hiking boots, and has the grace to say sympathetically to my porter, "Tell her not to go so fast!"

It was bliss to arrive at the inns in the evening. Innkeepers lived on the ground floor. Bedrooms, added on for guests, were wooden cubicles on the second floor, often with a window that offered a panoramic view of the Himalayan peaks. Somewhere

Following an old man with the legs of a runner up the Kali Gandaki Gorge.

near was a tap of cold running water; hot water arrived in a bucket, on request. Toilets were a slit in a dirt floor or porcelain set into the floor. I found that the inns often looked poor and shabby from a distance, but were clean, orderly and comfortable when you entered. I never went to bed hungry, cold or dirty.

The best thing about the inn food was that it's all fresh, cooked to order. Someone is always chopping veggies in the corner of a Nepali kitchen, while some form of *chapati* bread is puffing up in the outdoor oven. Purna and Ram ate *dal-bhat* twice a day, but my favorite was a Swiss *rosti*, a potato pancake, stuffed with diced onions, carrots, celery and cabbage.

Even better than the food and warm bed, however, was the chance to enter the world of our hosts, to sit on a mat by the light of a kerosene lamp and talk.

"Has she been married?"

"Has she children?"

"Is she alone?"

Purna and Ram answered these questions for me every night by the kitchen fire, as we compared notes about our homes, children, and the role of women.

In the first inn, at Nagdanda, we were sitting at a trailside table, sipping the spicy Nepali tea, when an old woman grabbed the day-pack I was trying to mend and finished the chore. In the last, at Kogbeni, our rooms overlooked the stable where the Patriarch of the house spent all morning sharpening a stick of soft wood to a fine point. About lunch time he tethered his bullock to a post and pierced the nose of the howling animal. Next morning he led it out to work by its new iron ring.

In all its elements, the constant on the trail is change. Its surface can be mud, or gravel, or pine needles, or rocks or a stream bed. At the start, just north of Pokhara, we begin at 2,600 feet in a lush, green, steamy land where banana and pipal trees flourish. On the second day we push up 4,000 feet to Ulleri, then down again, all the next day, my hot knees shaking. At Tatopani we pick up the Kali

Gandaki River and, from now on, we will never be far from its wild flow — muddy and frothing in the fall after the monsoon rains.

As we move steadily upward, tourists thin out and, when I least expect it, I start catching up with Ram. He keeps looking back to find me matching his stride. It's easy now to stay high, sniffing conifers in the crisp air, even as the majestic Dhaulagiri — at more than 26,000 feet — looms over my left shoulder.

Many hill tribes pass as we climb, the women a gallery of vivid beauty, in their burgundy velvet jackets and baroque gold nose-rings, their necks and chests covered with luxuriant strands of yellow, red, and orange beads. As they glide past in their long wrap skirts, the colors knock you out, and the faces look you steadily in the eye, full of pride and curiosity.

From Marpha (8,750 feet) onwards, the barren hills, prayer flags and faces are pure Tibetan. Jomsom is gray and somber, perched on the edge of an alluvial plain. A horseman in a fur hat with the features of a Tartar crosses the wide river bed, and boys sell ammonite fossils by the road, relics of a time when this region was an ocean floor. The imprint caught in the ebony stone is a prawn-like mollusk — and revered locally as "a mark of the gods."

Kogbeni, as far north as we go, is a stark, forbidding place. Road barriers, cutting off any travelers into Mustang, are just up the road. My wool hat is pulled down against the fierce wind, and Ram has made himself a turban from my warm scarf. We're on our tenth day when we arrive — an age away from the muggy sensuality of Pokhara where we started.

From here, I take a day trip on a balky white horse up another 990 meters, to Muktinauth, a pilgrimage site mentioned in the Hindu Vedas where a spring and a flame of natural gas — hidden in a crawl-space cave — have offered, for 1500 years, eternal salvation to believers. I couldn't have climbed this high, but I'm not too weak to get off my nag on the way down and pull him home after me.

Retracing to Jomsom, we fly out next day. I have a slight tussle retrieving the treasured cashmere I'd handed over to Ram on the

"Namaste! *Mother!*"

chilly slopes. (A regular visitor told me later: "Never lend any of your clothes. That means you don't need them.") On the plane, his first flight, Ram sits just ahead of me, turning his head ever so cautiously, for fear he might tip the plane over too far, peering down on the thin, white ribbon of river as we whiz back in a half hour over terrain it has taken us a week to traverse.

I dream of *chautarra* rest stops now — the best place on the road to connect with other Nepali travelers, one to one. You sit down — tired — and they are tired too. They sit on their haunches and smoke. You mop your neck and put suntan lotion, Number 15, on your nose. They all want a dab, and you pass it around. They offer you a slice of melon. Maybe there's even another breathless old woman with white hair and lines in her face, an *aamaa* like you. She gives you a great, deep laugh and asks how old you are. When you finally get up to move on, you each bow your head towards the other, and — this time — "*Namaste*! Mother!" sounds exactly right.

After my high in the Himalayas, I cut the cord and rent my house for three months, fly from Kathmandu to Delhi, and on into Kashmir. The U.S. State Department's advisory against travel by road across the restless Punjab tells me that if I want to see the contested Jewel-in-the Crown, I'd better do it before its volatile border with India is closed.

The four day trip up the Jehlum river out of Srinagar is bolder than anything I had yet done — and my first close-up encounter with the Muslim world.

Blindly, I follow a homesick opportunist back home and find the arrangement a fair trade.

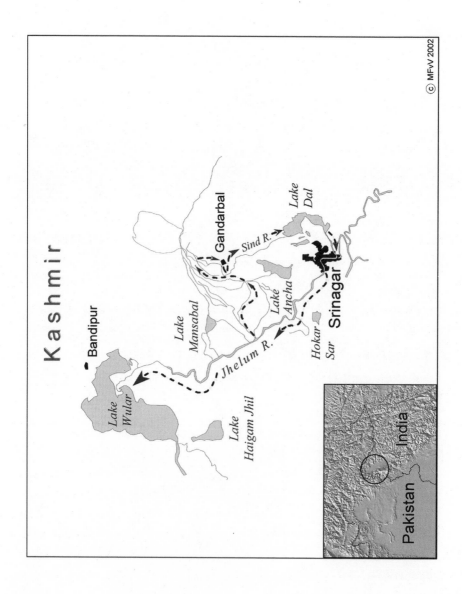

5   Away from the Glitz:

Kashmir

From the houseboat, "Argonaut," Dal Lake, Srinagar:

Even with the sliding lattice-work screens open on both sides of the narrow room, it was an airless night in the vale of Kashmir. My floating neighbors on the left are arguing, on the right, celebrating. Restlessly, I doze off, my head still busy packing and my thoughts anxious.

I wake up in a sweat, mumbling to myself. "You must be crazy! Going off with three unknown Muslim men! How could you have drifted into such an arrangement?"

It was simple, really. The artificiality of the houseboat scene was wearing thin. The indolent days had become too sweetly contrived — a surfeit of honey. I felt as if I were living inside the frame of a Persian miniature. I'd been there a week — long enough.

The days have been leisurely and carefree. From the houseboat in the early morning, Farouk would paddle me off to the vegetable market in his wooden *shikara* boat named "The King of Diamonds." From underneath its gold-tasseled canopy I could peer out at a traffic jam of other boats, each piled high with a luscious crop, lime-green beans in one, purple cabbage in another. At noon, we might cross over to his cousin's *papier mache* shop or visit the Shalimar Gardens. After supper, he'd take me out again to watch the pink light fade behind the white mosque Hazratbal, musk floating in the air, cardamon seeds in the tea, and flattery on the lips of every trader.

Everything in Srinagar, a city of 450,000 and the hub of Kashmir's tourist economy, is for the pleasure of the visitor. During the short summer "season", it is his open purse that keeps the community going through the frozen winter months when Kashmir has its beauty all to itself.

Now, in August, a perfunctory knock on the houseboat's gate announces Nick, the tailor, who steps up onto the porch. He sits on the floor and puts out soft samples made from the wool of the *pashmina* goats who live in the mountains above. He is hoping "to measure Madame for a cashmere suit."

At another hour, Omar's *shikara* pulls alongside ours. Just as I'm wondering about the lump in the hold, covered by a drab cloth, he whisks it away to reveal a dazzling jewelry shop. "Does Madame prefer rubies or emeralds?" he asks. At any hour on Dal Lake, a girl with the largest eyes in the world, may reach out to you with a pink lotus blossom, just pulled from the bottom.

"The price?"

"As you like."

On the "Argonaut," I am sinking into carpets, leaning into velour cushions and waited on by six men who glide through the rooms as soundlessly as the boats through the water. Each one is mulling over the possibilities for exchange — and profit — as is Abdul Kalich, who sits barefoot in the corner of the porch, watching as I study the map in my guide book.

"Are you thinking of traveling farther?" he asks me.

"Friends have told me I must not miss Gulmarg."

He mutters and makes a face. "It's just a hill, and full of tourists. I could show you the real Kashmir, up the Jehlum river, higher and cooler to see village life."

I am swayed by such promises. Villages, I know, are where 80 percent of India lives, yet few visitors have access to them. Abdul spreads HIS map out on the table while I drink Indian gin, and listen to his proposed itinerary as the sun goes down. It's tempting, but he comes without credentials.

"I couldn't go alone!" I insist. "Others will have to be found."

"No problem," he responds expectedly. "I will find someone."

I don't give it much more thought until the next day when, all smiles, he tells me:

"Allah is with us! They will come at seven tonight, to talk."

"A couple?"

"No. Two men."

I suppose that will do, but I had thought another woman along would be more comfortable. But Abdul gives me no time to hesitate; we must spend the day making arrangements. We will travel by *shikara* and camp out in tents — four days on the river. He must shop today for supplies, so we can leave tomorrow. I give him an advance, without realizing I am not quite ready to make a commitment. I await the evening in some suspense.

Later on, I notice that native men are puttering around the dock, which I don't pay much attention to until they go into a huddle with Abdul. After a bit, he comes over and tells me we can leave "next day."

"But I must meet the others," I say emphatically, suddenly wary. "Where are they?"

Two Kashmiri youths extricate themselves from the group and stand respectfully in front of me.

"I am called Nazaramid," the tall one says.

"Marajhen," announces the younger, shy one.

"They are strong paddlers," breaks in Abdul. "I am guide and cook." Suddenly, I am in an awkward corner. I don't want to insult them, but this is NOT what I had in mind!

"Where are the other . . . Westerners," I ask weakly — "other tourist-travelers?"

Paddling away up the Jehlum, "the boys" in the stern.

"No more room in the boat," explains Abdul. "For you, not comfortable with more people." In slow motion, I begin to understand.

I weigh the odds: He's taking me into his own territory. He will know how to get me there, and back, safely. What do I have that he might want? A passport, some Travelers' checks, a camera, a tape-recorder. I am too old for a harem. I can't think what would be in it for any of them to rob me or hurt me. They need my business; they need my references.

But it isn't sudden logic that reassures me. I look into Abdul's face, into all their faces. There's not a sinister slant in any of them. I like their faces.

Now, on the eve of departure, I go over all this again during my wakeful reprise, and a shrug delivers the verdict. I snuggle down into the hard, damp pillow and go back to sleep solidly, as the soggy night fades away.

DAY ONE on the Jehlum River:

We embark the next afternoon with fierce swiftness, the boys sitting in the rear, pulling hard, in unison, on their heart-shaped paddles. Abdul Kalich sits in the middle of the 20 foot boat, while I have the front half to myself. We are separated by a board that is his serving table and my backrest. A crude awning is our roof, making a flimsy covering over the central part of the boat. Gold/yellow curtains can be pulled around me, separating me from "the crew," giving me a little privacy — for changing clothes, personal grooming and napping. Otherwise, I have breezes and views on all four sides, sleeping-bag bolsters at my back and stretch-out space for my legs in front.

Abdul Kalich is in charge. I have already found out that he is 31 years old, the father of two and, more significantly, that the place we are headed for is his home. He shows me his kerosene stove, his lantern and — man of the world that he is — the bottled water and toilet paper he knows I will ask for. Facilities are casual: "Ask me when you want to stop," Abdul has told me. This turns out to be easy. He puts a plank out, helps me across it, points in the direction of a wall or a clump of trees and waits for me to return. Sometimes, if we are in a village, there is an actual facility, but it is usually unpleasant.

In the first hour after we pass through Dal Gate and follow the Jehlum west, then north, the river is fast. We fly downstream under the nine bridges of the city, our curtains flapping, our necks craning to catch the three-storied brick and wooden houses of the old city and some of its most interesting mosques. The houseboats we pass are not for tourists, but barges called *doongas*. Looking through their open windows, we catch glimpses of bronze pots on the wall, quilts piled high and scenes of Kashmiri domesticity.

From this point on, we mark the day by the Muslim Call to Prayers. These remain the defining, plaintive music of the Muslim realm. At 4:30 PM a man on the left bank turns to the east and throws himself forward on the ground. The sun is low and hot on the river, which here exudes a putrid smell. I keep my hands in the boat, but on the steps along both sides of the river, it's the hour for the evening clean-up. Young men strip and soap; children splash and swim. Women come down to wash their pots. Enormous terra cotta vessels and glistening brass pots are at ease on their heads, as they stand, in postures of indescribable grace as our boat slowly passes. One enters, center-stage, like a goddess, wearing pink; set off by the feathery green of the poplars behind her, she is a vision.

"Yes," says Abdul, "our women ARE beautiful. Like apples."

By 6:30, dusk is moving in and Abdul is cooking. The paddlers are slowing down, and we are all drinking beer and listening to a tape of Indian music. From a mosque hidden in the trees nearby, the 7:30 Call interrupts us and puts our day to rest. We pull alongside a *doongas* family that Abdul recognizes. For protection, he tells me.

Abdul lights our lantern and, across the board between us, passes me a white napkin and silverware, then a plate of curried mutton stew, rice, tiny cubed carrots with a touch of chili, and one

Inside the 'shikara,' Abdul Kalich smoking, curious villagers on the bank.

perfect banana. In the back, the crew eat a spicier version and talk in their own language of Urdu.

Afterwards, I opt to sleep in the boat, rather than on shore. Abdul asks if he may put his bag down in front of me — so the boys can have more room in the back. Feet to head, each enwrapped in our own thoughts, we face a noisy night on the river. We hear every whimper of the baby next door settling down, then, from the woods, the Late Show dog chorus. In the deepest part of the night, I part the curtains to look out at a new moon and bright stars.

DAY TWO starts much too soon.

At 4:30 AM, a song to the new day rises over the water. Thank God, I'm not a Muslim and expected to respond!

It is light as we move out on a snaky path through a shaded canal, across a garden of water lilies, into cool, clear, deep Lake Mansabal. We buy five pomphret fish from a boy with a bicycle in his boat, and I put on my one-piece black tank suit and dive over the side, which seems to embarrass my male guides. Too much show of skin, I suspect; Kashmiri women bathe fully dressed — in their pantaloons and long-sleeved shifts. Over breakfast of the fish, which tastes vaguely muddy, I admire Abdul's cool drawstring pants and floppy shirt, all one material, a cotton. In no time, the boys are paddling again furiously, this time to the dressmaker.

We tie the boat up at a small dock and are making our way toward the side street of a lakeside village. Five men sit in a cubicle, high off the dirt lane, no doubt to stay above the monsoon-season floods. They sell soap, sugar and fabric. Abdul, the interpreter and tastemaker, suggests a conservative small print, leafy effect, a gray line on white. They know how much to cut, so with this under my arm, we move on to the next shop, the one with the sewing machine. I step up off the street and am measured there as the village passes by, with many eyes watching, and some stopping to comment. My clothes will be ready the next day, they tell me.

"Will you take our picture?" they ask, seeing my camera. The workers in this shop all line up, but three shots later, it appears someone has been forgotten. A rush of men crowd up the stairs which I had not noticed before. The house has a second floor with a porch above the shop. They carry an old man out from a back room — the patriarch — to sit for a portrait with his sons and grandchildren. As he steadies himself to stand up, straight and still, it's a solemn moment.

In the afternoon, we visit Abdul's village, called Hajhen, population of about a thousand. At a place that looks like all the others, we moor on the river and walk through the woods, to emerge on a dirt Main Street. I meet the whole tribe, but the high point is the school teacher who greets me, jubilantly, in straightlaced English: "I hope you enjoy your visit to Hajhen."

After, that, I tell how old I am many times and take dozens of pictures of men grinning insanely before the interiors where they work. It's a boisterous hour, my first in a public place in Kashmir where no one asks for anything. On the grounds of the "sights" of both India and Kashmir, begging is what one comes to expect; here, not even the kids have their hands out for sweets.

"We are not a poor village," Abdul tells me. "We have brick houses . . . some brick houses." Nevertheless, during the tourist season, Abdul must leave his family and travel to Srinagar to work on the houseboats. It's been two months since he's seen his wife, Nura, and their children.

Abdul Kalich lives in his mother-in-law's house, across the lane from the river, behind a willow fence, through a gate and into a mud courtyard with a cow, a goat and chickens. When we arrive, it is twilight and a clap of hands dispatches someone to spread out a carpet in front of the house. Over this is laid a quilt and, on top of the quilt, one pillow. I am motioned towards it, and Abdul comes to sit beside me. Another handclap brings his seven-year-old son with the *hooka*/waterpipe for his father.

Nora and the family speed us onward with a gift of her chicken curry — at the riverbank.

After a while, his mother-in-law comes to sit beside me. From the outdoor kitchen, we are served spicy tea and *nan* bread. Then one by one, the women of the house take turns coming to sit with me. Nura could be Abdul's sister; it's the same face. She is five months pregnant and carrying a feverish two-year-old on her hip. I meet an "adopted" daughter and many cousins, some of the 13 people who sleep in the four rooms of the house. To cover what I take as awkward silences, I attempt woman-talk, praising Abdul's omelets, asking questions. But my hosts have no such compunctions. Mostly, we sit in what Kipling calls the "uncounted Eastern minutes," watching night fall over the river. Snatches of conversation echo through the courtyard and interrupt the wheeze of the *hooka*. Abdul inhales deeply, anxiously cradling his pale daughter as we settle into the humid darkness together, whacking away at the first mosquitoes.

When I wake up in the boat on **DAY THREE**, some sense tells me I am not alone.

Pulling back the curtains, I find a dozen children peering down from the top of the river bank, waiting for me to get up. On stage, brushing my teeth over the side, I try to keep ugly white drips off my chin. Indians, at their morning toilet, discreetly rub twigs between their teeth.

Nura comes down to speed us onward with a gift of her chicken curry, and we are off on a quick backtrack to the Boutique, to collect my pantsuit. When I emerge from my dressing room space, many cheer, and I sit lighter in the boat, from now on barefoot, with my wide, soft trousers as flimsy and yielding as the summertime breezes.

By now, it's clear we won't be camping out in tents. The *shikara* — cleaner, cooler, drier than the earth — and supplying us with protection from both the actual and the imagined creatures of the night, becomes our refuge.

In spite of the beauty, we become aware of the daily struggle for survival that surrounds us too. In the morning mist, men of all ages crowd into their boats, dredging the silt, which they use as a building material, from the river bottom. One man stands, poling; one, with a long-handled shovel, digs, while another, who holds a strong cord attached to the shovel, is the human pulley who lifts the shovel towards the mountain of mud rising in the center of the scow. We see young women, waist-high in water, in their bright prints, groping with their feet on the shallow bottom, for twigs brought in by the current. They will dry these and use them for kindling. We watch a stream of girls, often children, race us along the river banks, heading for home with baskets of grass on their heads, some weighing as much as fifteen pounds. We stop to talk to Amina who makes the 12 kilometer round trip daily, to collect fodder for the family animals. She collapses with laughter when I try to copy her and can't even stand up with a half-empty basket on my head.

On our last night on the river, paddling toward Gandarbal, not quite in the dark, I ask Abdul about his arranged marriage. He was 20 and his father was dead, he told me, when his older brother, the head of the family now, told him he had found him the perfect wife. Unconvinced and unenthusiastic, Abdul said he would think it over, but got her name and her village. Taking the next day off, he went to see for himself.

"Who is this Nura?" he asked.

When she was pointed out, he approached her and managed a casual conversation. Suddenly suspicious, she wanted to know, "Who are you anyway — taking all my time!!?"

"I am your husband."

Her face went red and she ran away in a rage, screaming back at him, "No, you're NOT!"

"I liked her too much," he explained.

After this meeting, they saw each other for a year before the ceremony — but never alone.

"It is not like in America," he confided. "She must stay home and not let other men see her."

That night, for the first time on our riverboat, with my three kohl-eyed, black-skinned protectors, I sleep hard. After three days "up the Jehlum" looking for "the real Kashmir," I have become conditioned — to the barking dogs, the mosquitoes, the rocking of the boat, the wake-up cries of the muezzin — even to the occasional kick of Abdul's nocturnal reflexes, to which I respond with an automatic, wifely kick back. We have become an almost-family, born of mutual advantage. Abdul wanted to go home; the boys needed a job — and were, as advertised, "strong paddlers" — and I wanted a peek at village Kashmir, at the river's edge.

On **DAY FOUR,** we begin to retrace our path.

Now traveling with the racing current, the journey back to Srinagar is swift. Our boat slips through a narrow, overgrown canal whirring with kingfishers who have nested in the deep holes along the ravine. When we shoot out of this dim draw, we are out again in open water — owls, blinking into sunlit pools choked with lotus blossoms.

I don't think I'll ever forget the fluid beauty at the heart of Kashmir. Any river trip has its monotonous moments; but the fast-paced, sudden encounters of form and light and color that shot across our bow are still with me. Close, almost too close, another scow crosses in front of us as we are about to reenter Dal Lake. A chalk-white chicken stands tall into the wind astride the cabin, its feathers ruffled back like a matron's feather-boa. A breathtaking nymph crouches in the stern, maneuvering her charge with all speed, back to the lake's commercial hub. As she ducks her head into the long folds of her bright red scarf, clearing our boat by inches, I crane my head backwards to memorize that picture before it passes out of sight.

Abdul Kalich, the consummate trader — always watching — grins. He can see by my face that he has delivered his promises.

It hasn't been so much a linear journey, as a step through the curtains backstage away from the glitz, where he has introduced me to the players without their makeup. His kinsmen had not charmed one single cobra for their visitor. They had simply offered themselves, with the assurance it would be enough.

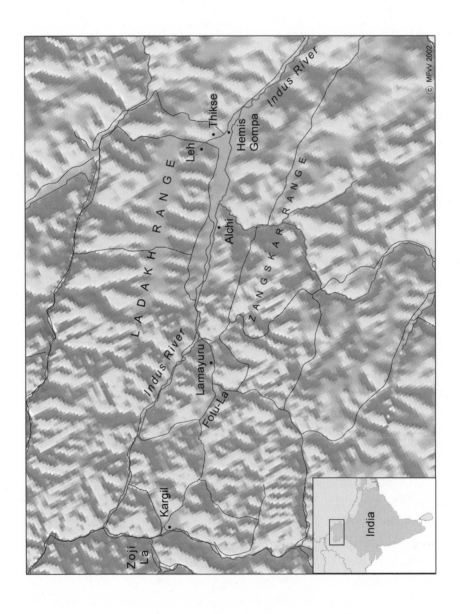

6   Letter from Ladakh

I had seen my first Tibetans circling the sacred pilgrimage site, the second century Mahabodhi Temple at Bodh Gaya, Bihar province, on my first trip to India. The open radiance of their faces, their entirely handwoven clothes, the rough, massive turquoise and coral jewelry that both men and women hung all over themselves, the indomitable vitality they threw off, like electricity, as they walked and talked and laughed, all told me I was looking at a rare mixed hybrid of human/animal magnetism.

These steppes survivors, whose natural habitat was the most unforgiving land in the world, had something wild, almost superhuman about them, and their faith, their dependence on their gods, was in their eyes. I couldn't wait to see more of them in their own country.

In 1985, when the Chinese-built Friendship Highway from Nepal to Lhasa, opened, I started looking for a way to go. In July 1986 I got there with a travel company based in Berkeley, a group of 16, led by an American living in Nepal, who spoke Tibetan. By then, Tibetans had endured the Cultural Revolution and 27 years of occupation. *Han* Chinese by the thousands had been imported and put in leadership positions. Native Tibetans, a distinctive culture, were a third-class minority in their own country. It seemed so outrageous that all I wanted to do after I returned was make political speeches and march in front of the Consulate; I couldn't write about it objectively.

"Go to Ladakh instead," the traveling-world told me, "if you want to see the culture intact and Tibetans thriving." The Indian government, I knew, had long ago welcomed Tibetans in Jammu-Kashmir province, a high desert plateau, not unlike their homeland, as well as giving asylum in 1959 to the Dali Lama and his entourage in the fading British Hill Station of Dharamsala.

During my long summer away in 1986, I grabbed my chance. After I returned to Srinagar, Kashmir from the Jehlum River journey ("Away from the Glitz," Chapter 5), I was at the exact crossroads from which the buses leave twice a week for the 698 mile crossing over the Zoji La into Leh, the capital of Ladakh. Furthermore, it was summer: the roads would be open until October.

This is where I parted from Abdul Kalich, my Kashmiri guide. He got me the ticket, bought me some *chapati* bread and bananas, and firmly led me to a seat next to the only other Westerner on the bus. She turned out to be Lili, a delightful multilingual Portuguese woman from Paris, traveling with her teenagers, a boy and a girl. They were careful, independent travelers; her husband was at home, making animated films, in which the whole family were employed part-time, but she took their children traveling whenever she could. We were all instantly empathetic.

In spite of the diversion of good company, however, we arrived, like most tourists, sleepless from our overnight in Kargil (a truly unendearing place) and the 4:30 AM wake-up call, with bones and nerves shaking from the two-day ordeal. Indian buses have shock absorbers that don't absorb, and the boulder-strewn road cuts across mountains that rise thousands of feet up from a river bed. Still, it's a mistake to fly. The only way to see how Leh fits into its stage-set is to enter the valley by its arduous roadway.

When the traveler has climbed by cranky bus up beyond the tall, thin Kashmiri pines, through the fingers of the glaciers, and watched the land colors change from green to ocher to starkest gray, he has, in a sense, attended a rehearsal for Leh Valley. We passed adobe-brown dunes that in the evening light reminded me of the sheen and shape of a lion's flank; and no one could miss the remarkable pink forms of wind-eroded rock called "the Red Sea," near Lamayuru. After crossing the highest pass, the Fotu La (13,430'), we looked down into the Indus River Valley, where the Hindu Vedas were born. My dirty bus window had much to reveal about the forces that have shaped this high desert.

Historically, the inhabitants of this region like to think of themselves as part of the old Kingdom of Ladakh, independent and safe from foreigners, protected as they are by the Karakorum and Kalish ranges on the north and east, by the Great Himalayan range on the south. In fact, over the centuries, the country has been invaded by Tibet, Mogul India and Kashmir. Part of India since the Independence in 1947, Ladakh remains a nervous border where India meets China and Pakistan. Indian military garrisons are in evidence, and boundaries continually in dispute. On the other hand, its violent legacy and its myriad cultural strands are one of the aspects that make it so entrancing; the smells, sounds, shapes and turbulence of the ancient Asian Silk Route are never far away.

June to September is the High Season in Leh. Bulls wander down the middle of the dusty main street, playfully locking horns. Women — decorated with turquoise and silver and sometimes wearing a top hat called a *tibi* and the long wool *coss*, brightly sashed — sit on the sidewalk in front of mounds of cauliflower, peas-in-the-shell, turnips, tomatoes, apricots and potatoes. An old Tibetan, whose hair is stiff with Yak butter, sits on the corner talking to his beads. Faces from the ancient trade routes of Yarkand (now China) and Baltistan (now Pakistan) mingle with the Mongolian-Ladakhi faces, and with the Muslims from Kashmir, and Hindus of every caste from India. Tea, barley and raw sugar are sold in bulk from open burlap sacks, and the local housewife is wooed by displays of shiny aluminum pots, hand-printed yardage and whisk brooms.

An exotic tribal family crosses our path as we go over the Zoji La.

In some respects, it's a vigorous scene from the Middle Ages — except for the Kashmiri Art and Curio shops, and items found in the stores such as toilet paper, Pond's Cold Cream, vitamin "C" and stereo cassettes — dead giveaways that "Little Tibet" is no longer cut off from the outside world.

The tourist, in summer, is everywhere visible, flashing his long, pale legs below his hiking shorts, announcing his identity a block away by his hat brim, money belt and camera case. Those who try to merge — by wearing the Punjabi pants and tunic, the sari-wrap skirt, or the towel turban — look even more out of place. Flesh pink is the wrong color in India.

At the bank, the line for cashing travelers' checks straggles down the sidewalk, and every evening the bus from Srinagar drops dozens of travelers at the tourist office. Shortly, they will be panting up the hills out of town (at 10 to 12,000 ft.) searching for the perfect Guest House, hotel or campground. Tourists are lined up at the stamps counter at the post office and outside the restaurant with the best rep for safe food. In the bazaars, they practice the Byzantine art of bargaining and find the 300 rupees ring can usually be purchased for less than 100. Buses are SRO and jeep taxis booked ahead, jolting visitors through the rocky desert, to Hemis and Thikse to see the hilltop monasteries with the serene golden Buddhas and the dark, skull-crowned gods of destruction. At Sabu, travelers go to watch the Healer suck the troublesome poison/venom from the patient or to Shey, hoping to catch sight of the Oracle in trance.

During my first few days in Leh, with my new friends bonded by the rough bus ride, I lived in a hotel with a flush toilet, for 150 rupees ($12.50) a day. Like the countless others, we rushed out into the streets from morning till 7:30 dark, sniffing mud, musk and dung. We visited the huge red and gold prayer wheel near the original gate to the city and, in the bazaar, bought a human skull inlaid in silver, a relic of Tantric Buddhist sacrifices. One day we squeezed onto a bus for Alchi and traveled a day to see the intricate, 11th Century woodcarvings that decorate its portals. Another day, we were buffeted about when a visiting *Rimpoche* (Head Lama) came to pray in the local temple. The crowd went crazy as his jeep passed by, with the opened, tasseled, orange parasol on top, which showed the man himself was inside. We zipped through the valley monasteries so fast that, in my mind, they were all one sprawling city of *gompa*/temples with the features of each fading in and out, like a two-projector slide show.

Then something happened that changed my visit to Ladakh: the flush toilet in my hotel stopped flushing, and I and my friends moved up the road to a Ladaki family Guest House where, for 20 rupees a night ($1.66), I discovered another Leh.

Here, my flat-roofed adobe sits on a hill a mile out of town above the dirt road that leads towards the terraced farmlands. Steps go up, through a gate in a stone and mud wall, to its upper level where rows of healthy vegetables surround the path and yellow sunflowers guard the house. Cool passageway steps inside climb to my room where I look out over the garden, the wall, the street and across the poplars and willows on the other side of the valley mountains, to the sharper, white peaks that are the final etching against the cobalt sky. The roof of my 13 feet by 13 feet space is supported near the room's center by a fat poplar column, simply and eloquently carved at the top in a scallop design. The ceiling is made up of smaller beams, interwoven with branches, all in the same warm, blond wood. It's one of the loveliest "skies" I've ever slept under.

Downstairs, guests take meals in the center of a Ladakh house: the kitchen. Chung-Li and Norbu, a young couple without children, are in charge, part of a large extended family who visit often, their exuberant greeting *'jullay'* echoing through the house at all hours. We sit in an "L" along the two walls, on the thick carpets which have been placed in front of low tables. The embossed iron and brass stove dominates and is where Chung-Li presides; on cool mornings she wears Western pants and sneakers under her long brown wool dress.

For breakfast (six rupees), she gives us *chapati* bread, *tsampa* porridge or eggs; for dinner, a freshly made soup and a vegetable stew with rice or noodles, or the Tibetan *momo*, vegetables wrapped in a thin, decorative pasta, served with a chili tomato sauce. A sweet pudding and camomile tea with cardamen seeds ends the 10 rupee meal. When a guest departs, he is sped onwards with a glass of the local barley beer, *chang* — lemon pop, with a kick.

Facilities in this accommodation are basic and clean. There is no non-functioning toilet, only a slit in a tidy, dirt floor that drops into a composting toilet below — and no spigots that leak all over your feet as you bend over the basin, a common occurrence in India. Chung-Li washes her clothes, as well as her long black hair in the run-off spill from the glaciers that pass in front of her gate, along a narrow canal. Further upstream, she and Norbu collect water in thin metal tanks they strap on their backs and carry up to the roof of their house. From there, the water feeds down through pipes to supply them with cold water for showers and washing. Hot water is delivered by bucket — with a half-hour's notice — heated on the stove which is fired with dried dung cakes. Beds are thin pads over a stiffly-webbed cot that's smothered in heavy quilts. Electricity, as it does in the "best" hotels, comes on five days a week from 7:30 to 11:00 PM — usually. There are candles in every room and, on each landing, a kerosene lamp, ready to be lit.

Lili and her brood move on in a couple of days. With promises that I will come to Paris and they will take me to Portugal, we part. Completely on my own, at last, I nestle into my second-floor observatory, where I am occupied, happy and mesmerized for another ten days, watching the turn of the day outside my window.

The day in Leh begins with the 4:40 Muslim Call to Prayer. In my room, the next sound I hear is the resident Buddhist monk in the cubicle next to me, droning his deep, humming prayers, in

Sanskrit, I imagine. People are out early, carrying grass on their backs to their livestock or, with a shovel, collecting dung. Through the day, all ages, even four-year-olds, squat on the stones in the cold streams and beat their clothes clean. In the fall, which we are moving into, out on the tiered fields, farmers thresh rice and barley in the late afternoons, singing as they swing the scythe, the high-keyed rounds of a work song that must be hundreds of years old. Children start moving home from school about 4:00 PM, the boys wrestling their way along the roads, just like the bulls downtown. Every evening at dusk, I realize men are transferring their ponies from polo fields in town, out to grazing land, galloping them, fast, through the streets under my window. Later, donkey bells — almost inaudible— and the beat of drums — drift in from a long way off. I have to sit very still at my window and quiet my breathing to hear them.

There's a strong ecology movement here in Leh and concern that tourism is breaking down the gentle life, which so perfectly reflects the religion of the majority of its people. The Buddhist doctrine of the interdependence of all living things has been acted out here — as a matter of course — for centuries.

With no crime and very little poverty, there's no doubt a lesson in Ladakh that so-called First World, "developed" countries could learn. There is certainly a rich personal experience for the visitor who can adjust his Swatch watch to a Ladakhi sundial, and his body to a Spartan mode. Long after the contemporary invader has left — and perhaps forgotten just what the murals at Shey looked like — he may still be able to recall — exactly as I can — the swishing sound of the old man's prayer wheel as it brushed past, almost touching my sleeve in the dark — and how low the stars were, almost touching too, as we trudged up the dirt road home.

By now I am beginning to sense something potent about being the anonymous single traveler, moving into town without a name-tag on or an advance guard of facilitators to check the mattresses and sanitation. An edginess exhilarates me. I am watchful, attentive, fully present in the moments — which seem to be drawn-out, with infinite potentials.

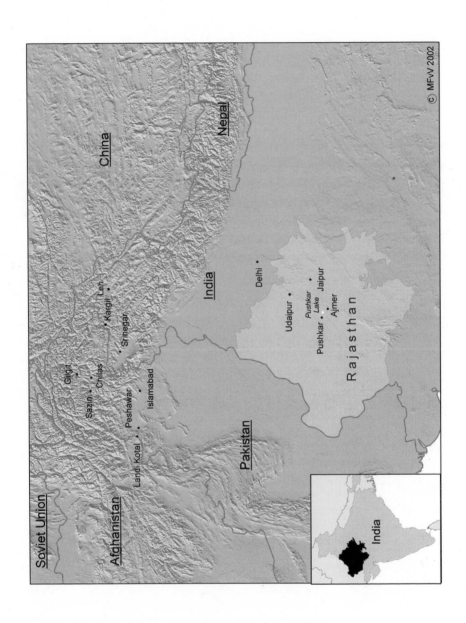

7 Full Moon Over Rajasthan:

Pushkar Camel Fair, India

As far back as the fifth century, Chinese traveler Fa Hein noticed pilgrims bathing in Pushkar's oval lake on the edge of the Thar desert, near Ajmer. Legend tells us, that it was here, while flying over his heavenly domain, that the great Lord Brahma, creator of all the universe and all lesser gods, absentmindedly dropped a lotus. Afterwards, holy waters sprang into being at the end of the lake, and as it became a popular pilgrimage site, bathing ghats were built so all good Hindus could step down to dip into the blessed waters. To this day, in all of India, the only Brahma temple is here at Pushkar.

Over uncountable years — on the full moon of the October/November lunar calendar, which Indians call Kartik Poornima, traders from all over northern India have gathered to celebrate the harvest with a vast camel and cattle fair. With money in their pockets, people traveled long distances in their camel-drawn carts to trade their livestock, to sell their goods and skills, to gossip, and to have a temple priest perform a potent, protective puja, before the lean winter to come.

Until after World War II, the camel fair remained a local event, of which only a few wandering Westerners knew. But by 1969, both the town and the fair had flourished so that Mrs. Chester Bowles, wife of the popular U.S, Ambassador to India, was quoted by the press as declaring: "You haven't seen India until you've been to the Pushkar Fair!"

Though livestock continued to be the main event, traders from Udiapur, Jaipur, and surrounding areas began to import other items: puppets, fabric, jewelry, and miniatures of Mughal princes painted on silk. Guest Houses multiplied, and tourism, having attracted thousands, had to provide facilities. Tent camps, dining pavilions, Indian food cooked on the premises, toilets and information desks became part of the scene — while the tattoo booth, once so popular with the villagers, disappeared, and camel rides for the westerner were featured.

Evolved by 1990 into a Tourist Trap of outrageous proportions, its reputation drew me, along with Sir Edmund Hillary, the Explorers Club, 7,000 foreign visitors and 15,000 camels to the fair in October 1991. My friends and I had brewed the plot six months earlier at a geriatric slumber party in Sausalito, California.

Olga, a retired lawyer, who spends half the year in Nepal running a foundation that rescues and nurtures street-children, invited me for dinner and the night. She wanted me to meet Preb, ex-Peace Corps teacher in Nepal, just passing through from Vermont. Olga thought we might have "something in common." It was the beginning of a triad connection which resulted in many fine times, the first, an agreement to meet, next season, in India, for the Pushkar Fair!

Many plans and faxes later, the three of us converge in Delhi, just as the Hindus and the Muslims are arming themselves over a temple-versus-mosque argument. The government of V.P. Singh, the current Prime Minister, is collapsing, and reliable news is scarce. Once in the Rajasthan area, our tourist-agency connections are anxious to reassure us that we can proceed. As we move in on Ajmer, we hear that road blocks and curfews have been put up en route, but having come this far, we cling to our determination to get to our humpy summit.

Thus on a certain Fall morning, we are driving through pre-dawn streets, glimpsing, here and there, doorways where filthy rags cover small, sleeping figures on the route to old Delhi Railway Station, which offers one of many never-to-be-forgotten Indian crowd-scenes. On the platforms, dozens of families have spread out rugs and blankets, and are at home, resting, chatting, eating, huddling around tiny fires and huge brass samovars that dispense Indian tea.

In time, the Pink City Express, our train to Jaipur, arrives, but as far as we can see, brings no first class cars. Irrationally, we feel reasonably secure with our first class tickets in hand, and our travel agent with us. He stands near, in a circle of conductors, expounding in his language as he waves our tickets, worth half a year's wages to the average Indian. As time passes, however, we notice that his brow is dripping with sweat. At the appropriate hour, when the train is scheduled to leave, it slowly pulls away from the station, and we are left dazed, clutching our bottled mineral water and our sturdy, locked luggage.

We have lost our train and squandered a morning, but the moon is still only three-quarters full and the fair hardly begun. We hire a car, which, in India, always comes with a driver, and dusk finds us all driving southwest down the Delhi/Jaipur road, fast-munching cucumber and chicken sandwiches packed by Claridge's hotel.

We pass everything: goats, pigs, camels, men camping in overturned trucks, road-crew workers with diamonds in their noses — all etched against the pink Rajasthan dirt, here and there scattered with mounds of rubble and the feathery kewar tree. In the background of almost every vista, the corn-husk shape of a Hindu temple or the dome of a mosque stands out on the horizon, symbols of the divisions that have almost kept us from getting here. With our luck holding out, we are waved on through the road block just before the 9:00 PM closing.

Thirteen kilometers down a gravel road, we suddenly see a mirage of lights slithering up Snake Mountain, across the lake from the town. There's a ferris wheel and florescent tubes of light across the road and, suddenly, the entrance: the gateway to a Maharaja's fort, made of raffia, its battlements flying the emblems of Rajasthan Tourism.

Once arrived, the driver lets us out among a labyrinth of tents, connected by newly-laid brick paths. As we search for our own accommodations, we pass what we think is a life-size decoration of a kneeling plaster camel — until we catch him blinking an eye at us. Up a lumpy dirt turnoff to Block F, we find our home, numbers 502 and 503. The rough, worn canvas looks as if four generations of nomads might have used it; inside, a thin rug covers the dirt and three cots are set out, sheathed in questionable bedding.

"Are these the 'deluxe' tents we paid for?" asks Olga, who once played sleuth for Drew Pearson. "Yes" comes the answer, "but not the 'Super deluxe'!"

We are too tired to protest. We have arrived, at last, and can't wait to crawl in and await the morning when the show continues. We have two more days before the morsel that the mouse nibbled out of our harvest moon disappears.

The next 48 hours are a psychedelic overkill of sensual bombardment. We move between the tourist tent-city, the country fair, the animal encampment, and the town built up around the holy waters. Wherever we go, we are harassed and jostled, our space, ears, and attention intruded upon. Beggars and bullocks prod us. Smells are mostly bad, air is foul, pavements hazardous and unhealthy. One needs two pairs of eyes on the streets of India, one to shut out, and one to let in.

No one coming for the first time from a First World country is ready for India — nor, in my experience, is one ever quite finished with it. But the Pushkar Fair manages to retain its original mix of the sacred and the profane. It IS the holy marketplace, with the color, imagination, contrasts and scale that only India brings forth; and it may well be, as Mrs. Bowles

The morning dip in the lake at Pushkar.

suggested, the truest microcosm of India that a stranger is likely to encounter.

Our tent city has 2000 tents, the super deluxe, 1000. Each has its own restaurants and facilities. In the toilet tent, an Untouchable sits on his haunches, nursing the fire under a huge pot of hot water which he pours into buckets in each shower stall: soap, toilet paper and clean towels are plentiful. Our accommodations cost us $40 a day each, including three meals, served buffet style in the big tent. The tourists are mostly middle-aged Europeans traveling in groups. They look far too much like ourselves for us to want to have anything to do with them.

The 4-H segment of the fair features booths with cows full of milk (the Yield contest) and goats and sheep trying to look their competitive best. Sleek, small black and white horses from eastern Rajasthan are brought into the central ring to be shown and sold. The camels come next. Preb, Olga and I meet at ringside for the event. A few are raced madly around the ring, a driver up on the hump, yanking the camel's red-tasseled halter so taut that the head is forced back and up into a tortured swan's neck curve, during which the animal manages to look both agonized and haughty.

On our first evening at dinner we sit with a mild man from Martinez, California who tells us, "It came over me quite gradually that I'm addicted to camels." We chew this over with our chapati, trying to do it sideways, as the camel does, practicing the weird bray we have been hearing. We wonder if this is why we are here.

I am certainly addicted to hanging around the camel camp at dawn. As soon as the sky changes from black to blue, I cross the mela where the improbable desert ships are spread out on the rolling sands — etchings dreamed a hundred times, but never before experienced. Some are sitting, munching on grass or oats, some are drinking from long water troughs, others feign sleep, or death. Wives and babies of the drivers are still wrapped in blankets. Bright eyes peek out as I pass in the overhanging mist. Some crude camel carts are being loaded with graceful, handmade wooden rakes. But soon the whole camp is stirring with action, vivid saris and turbans moving in every direction, the sun burning off the mist, the visitor exposed, and the precious moments of surreptitious watching, gone.

I tear myself away, along the road to the fair. Puppeteers of the Kavalia tribe — Ranas, Bhats — show their skills. In their hands, the elephant throws a garland over a temple lingam, two men duel with swords, another swings from his ankles on the flying trapeze. Back in the village, families apprentice their children to learn to carve the wooden puppet heads, make the costumes, and dramatize the old morality tales. I had seen several of these souvenir dolls back home, hanging lifeless as wall decorations, never imagining how they could "come alive" in the hands of a master puppeteer.

By myself now, with my pals off in different directions, I follow the crowds moving towards the lake and the prescribed morning ablutions. Men with towels over their shoulders keep me on track. As we reach the bathing ghats, women are selling strings of orange marigolds and lavender petals I can't name. Incense, drums, sacred cows, langur monkeys, and emaciated sadhus/holymen in orange flood the white, scalloped archways where, beyond, out in the polluted, blue water, priests in white beckon.

Blinking in the sun, I take off my sandals and move towards the water where a woman splashes about in her sari. Intending merely to observe and take pictures, if I can, I suddenly find myself confronted by a boy whose hands are full of flower petals and spices. Somehow managing to grab both my hands in his, he is saying, "Repeat after me, 'In the name of Brahma, Shiva, Vishnu.' " There isn't time to react; I just go along, feeling the petals fall in my hair. Next he makes a powder of all the herbs in his palm and puts the red tika dot on my forehead, exacting a small contribution "to the temple." Now I resemble all the other pilgrims at Pushkar.

Following the faithful around the lake, I see a tourist with a camera on tripod out on a sandspit, trying to catch the sadhus priest meditating there — so spare, so focused, so serene, clearly not of any world we know. At my feet, I look down, startled by a painted rock, which is moving. It turns out to be a yogi on a wheeled sled who has twisted himself into an inhuman knot — no usable arms or legs. I can hardly bear to look, but, when I do, he betrays his humanity by his blinking eye, like the camel on the footpath yesterday.

As I turn the corner, young women are cutting sugar cane and loading it onto carts. Silver triangles and stars are sewn onto their chiffon shawls and their arms are covered with gold jewelry. I bump against a Western man, who is reeking of expensive cologne and Gucci leather. He has allowed his immaculate head to be wrapped in a red and blue printed turban.

Suddenly I am exhausted by the highs and lows of India watching. Weary of every sensation, I head home along the lakefront, which is now flooded with the light of the full moon. "When will I ever be in such a strange and magical place again?" I muse, grateful that tent 503 awaits me and eager to regroup and compare notes with my traveling companions. It turns out Preb has been concentrating on photography and Olga has found the rug she was looking for; both visited the camel camp, but neither has a red dot on her forehead. We are all thrilled we have come.

On our final morning, we watch the Germans, French and Italians snapping the last photos of each other leaning against a smelly hump. As we wait for our taxi to the Jaipur train, which we hope will now be running, we watch the razzle-dazzle being dismantled. There is an element of mirage about Pushkar. Transactions have slackened, booths are disappearing before our eyes, and the only camels left are pulling carts piled with our dirty laundry. The nomadic caravans must have left at dawn, while we were sleeping. Pushkar is beginning to move back into the still center of itself — its universe appearing undisturbed.

When the taxi comes, the driver tells us a new Prime Minister has just been sworn in. He gives him three months in office. A convivial man, wanting to explain his country to foreigners, the driver tells us he is a member of the driver caste, worshipping Krishna who drove Arjuna's chariot. Krishna, we've found out, is a much-beloved aspect of Vishnu, while Arjuna is the national hero of India's longest-running Bestseller, the Bhagavad-Gita. Even the Lonely Planet hikers have it in their pack. Our driver's niche in life has been passed down to him, but within its confinements, he has made vast improvements in his circumstances. His grandfather drove only a cart pulled by a bullock, but now — like his sons, he tells us proudly — he drives a highly polished, sleek, black Ambassador sedan. We step into it and speed across the red desert dirt with a stinging, dry wind pushing us onward.

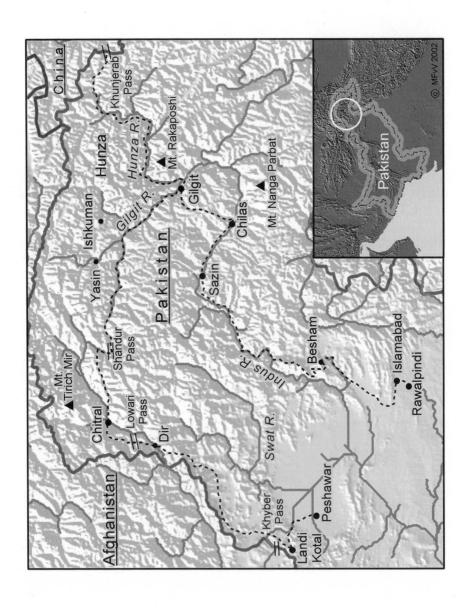

8   No Place for A Woman:

Pakistan, 1989

Before I left, the only good words that reached me about Pakistan applauded the mountains: "Spectacular and unspoiled!" But, everyone warned: "It's no place for a woman!"

That did it, fired my determination to go — to stand eye to eye and veil-less in the darkest corner of the Muslim world! To be in a place where a western woman was a stranger, where everything I'd been taught, everything that ordered my life, was on the bargaining table.

I talk Jane, into going with me. We had met on the Ukraine walk the year before (she was one of the "Over 50" Club!) and we agree to meet in Islamabad that fall of 1989.

At a westernized hotel — marble fountains in the foyer, romanticized Islamic art on the walls — we encounter a young Swiss couple who are also looking for a way to travel through the Northwest Frontier and confirm our notions that the best way to go is by jeep. They tell us about Sitara Travel, two blocks away, where we can rent a vehicle for hire.

When we get there, however, the manager, Zia, is clearly anxious about our plan.

"It is not safe for two madames to go to the northwest without a guide. Your driver will speak only Urdu."

Waiting for regime change, bus stop, Northwest Frontier province.

"Another person?" we protest, "That sounds too expensive!"

"For a 21-day jeep safari, the driver, the English-speaking guide, your accommodations — about 40 U.S. dollars a day, each."

"How can that be?" we ask in disbelief.

"Where they know him, your guide will get free meals and a bed, and naturally you will not pay for any rooms or meals for your driver."

"Why not?"

"He is a driver."

The driver's name, we find out, is Gophar; he's from Peshawar, married with five children. The morning we start out, he has on his only garment, an immaculate olive-drab, wool *shalwar-kameez*, the Punjabi uniform of baggy pants and a flapping tunic-shirt.

Fida Hussain, our guide from Hunza, we are told, is a cousin of the Mir (ruler). Small-boned, elegant and diplomatic, he wears the latest cut of European sports clothes and carries a small, stuffed briefcase.

Jane and I, hearing lumpiness is in order for women, each have two sets of the local dress, with a head-scarf that is more often around our necks than over our heads. With our essential toys — cameras, books and tape-recorders — our luggage is clumsily tied on the rear rack of the jeep with a thick frayed rope. Thank God we voted against bringing Jane's accordion and my laptop computer.

With our turquoise jeep open on both sides, we begin our journey. Jane and I take turns in the front, which we imagine is the best seat. Actually, the front is less dusty and the view never blocked, while the back seat is elevated and cooler. Riding a jeep turns out to be like riding a horse. You learn to swing into the bumps and grip with your gluteus muscles. After the first few days, we are so sore that we fancy we are exercising. "We must be losing weight!" Jane assures me.

On the southern end of the Karakoram Highway, we soon cross the mighty Indus — and will follow it north for another day and a half. As Gophar weaves our jeep around potholes like an Olympic slalom skier, we hang out on the curves and the river below seems to throw its energy towards us. There's a pool where a pure, aqua-blue stream enters the murky main, each color staying separate in the crotch before they mix together, as if on some artist's palette. Our spirits lift when the sun catches the white water or sinks into its angry, gray roar. We see few fishermen or boats. The rivers are just THERE, boring their way through the arid mountains, changing everything — changing us.

The jeep road, winding north through the Indus River gorge, slows us down internally, wheedles us to its own rhythms, begins to set in motion its own interference with our compulsive travel itinerary and our busy, talkative selves.

On the first day of our travels, we stop for the night at the Pakistan Tourist Development Corp (PTDC) Guest house at Besham, a bazaar town busy in summer, where the road from the Swat Valley joins the Karakoram. Our rooms are an oasis of cleanliness and simple, modern motel comforts with a balcony overlooking the Indus. We follow a path down to the sandy beach, where we treat our hot feet to a dip in the muddy, glacier flow.

I feel as if Gophar is driving us deeper into the past and think about the kind of people who first lived here and told the stories in the *Bhagavad Gita* (2500 > 1500 BCE). In the warm night, with the door open, I hear the river all night long and remember Krishna's description of the immortal soul:

> Unborn, undying,
> Never ceasing,
> Never beginning,
> Deathless, birthless,
> Unchanging forever.

The next day, still moving north, we notice how women sit by the side of the road and turn their backs as our jeep passes yanking their shawls up over their faces in gestures of annoyance.

The British — enmeshed in the politics of this area since the mid 18th century — left behind the tea-break, to which our party like everyone else in the region, strictly adheres. We always stop in mid-morning and again in mid-afternoon, wherever we are; the tea is hot, black, sweet, milky and comes in glasses. Sometimes we sit on the *charpoy*/rope beds that one sees along the road here and there, anywhere. Once we sat in a field with cows grazing nearby, and a dozen men came over to stare at us.

At Chilas, the next town north, on the dirt main street, we are besieged by scrappy ruffians, who fight each other to have their picture taken. Suddenly it is almost a mob, which pays no attention to our pleas for order. It is our first awareness that we are in a society where women's voices carry no authority. The female has been rendered virtually invisible and almost mute.

At 5000 feet, Gilgit is the only crossroads/market town of any consequence for hundreds of miles in any direction, and has been inhabited since the Third Century. I had read so much about its long and exotic history that I was surprised that its geography and general ambiance was still that of a boomtown ski-resort in Colorado — except for the signs in Sanskrit, the crowds on the street, all men in the Punjabi outfit, and a lot of goats running free. It is the administrative center of the North-west area and the trekking center of Pakistan — with an air-port, and Nanga Parbat, a magnificent 23,000 feet high, just around the corner.

As the home of the Gilgit Agency, set up by the British in 1877 when they feared Russia and China were moving in on their colo-nial interests, the town, during its heyday was the arena of what came to be called "The Great Game." There's not much left of this vibrant past when it was the loneliest outpost of the British Empire. Now, the practice polo match we go to see in the after-noon consists of native boys wildly racing unbroken ponies around a ring and seems to be put on for the tourists. As we walk home through the bazaar, we are the only women out on the streets among frowning men. "It offends good Muslim males," explains a bilingual Muslim I get to know, later, in Lahore, "to see women so immodest as to travel unaccompanied. 'Where is their father, husband, brother? Don't they have anyone in their family who thinks well enough of them to protect them?'"

At dinner, our Fida talks wistfully about his home in the Hunza Valley, where we will be tomorrow. Considered by Lord Curzon, one of India's most influential viceroys, to be "the ultimate manifestation of mountain grandeur," Hunza is about half the size of Connecticut, but contains more summits over 20,000 feet than there are over 10,000 feet in the entire Alps.

"Shangri-La," intones Fida, dreamily.

"It can't be that perfect!" we Americans tell him, stuck on our ideal of democracy. "No one has the vote!"

As our jeep laboriously climbs the 65 miles to Karimabad, Hunza's main town, the slopes grow perversely greener. The jagged mountains are, at every turn as we ascend, denser and a purer shade of white. In whatever direction we look, tiered gardens of wheat, maize and potatoes are held fast on their precarious ledges by dry stone walls. We turn off the main road which rises steeply up a series of ditches that pass for roads, through pinched lanes guarded by four-foot walls. We have so little room as we scrunch through that Fida keeps reminding us to "keep your elbows in!"

Our journey to Hunza takes us back in time to what was once an idealized feudal society, now, gradually, breaking up. Though the reputation of its people for longevity — once attributed to the high mountain air and a heavy diet of apricot pits — has been pretty much debunked, the place itself lives up to its reputation as a unique, Lilliputian jewel.

Geographically, Hunza appears implausible: a vertical desert that has been converted to productive land by irrigation channels — the oldest ones dug out by ibex horns — which filter the glacier runoff down from the mountains by a system of weirs. On the far side of the Hunza river, as we drive in, we can just make out the ribbon ledge, wide enough for a horse, which is the way Lord Curzon, and perhaps Marco Polo, entered. It was the only path into this 23-mile long valley, before the road was built in 1959.

Unlike the many displaced people in Pakistan who have relocated often, the man from Hunza knows exactly who he is and where he belongs. The mountains are his fortress; the Mir is his Father/ruler; and the Aga Khan, leader of all Ismaili Muslims everywhere, is his Imam — the 49th, whom they believe is directly descended from the Prophet Muhammad.

The first Hunza woman we meet along the road grabs Jane's cheap magnifying eyeglasses out of her hand and puts them on her own nose. Without any language between them, she indicates that she needs them more desperately than Jane. My adaptable fellow traveler agrees and turns them over.

The next Hunza woman we meet is the wife in the family inn at the top of the hill where we stay. On a porch overlooking the valley, she passes our dinner out from the kitchen: roasted baby potatoes, lamb stew cooked with kale, and tiny, chilled peaches. Afterwards, she emerges to greet us warmly. Her head is covered by a printed, blue kerchief, and her face is unveiled.

The Ismaili women of Hunza do not generally cover their faces or observe strict *purdah*, which requires that, as soon as girls pass puberty, they hide behind face-cloths with eye-slits and envelop themselves in a fabric which covers them from neck to ankle — called the *burqua*. In fact, the Ismailis are a lenient sect who pray three times a day, not five, and live a noncompetitive life, courtesy of the Aga Khan. He builds the schools, mosques and hospitals, asking a ten per cent, worldwide religious tax, "of those who can afford it."

We meet Kahrim, Fida's friend, the local historian who wonders how Hunza, ruled by one family since the 11th century, can make the transition from the middle ages to a developing, modern country. He fears the loss of family ties and "the embrace of newness." The Mir is now an elected official, but most Hunzakuts, he says, would rather have him continue to tell them what to do. They are used to a tiered system of government.

The Mir himself, we discover, lives just across the street from our inn. His "palace" is a sprawling affair with cabins on several levels where "guests" can stay. Through Fida, we arrange a couple of nights there. High tea is served in a 50-foot room on brass-topped tables in porcelain cups by old servants; sheep heads adorn the wall, along with a portrait of his ancestor, the infamous Ghazan Khan who, in 1868, murdered his father Ghazanfur by putting a fresh smallpox vesicle in his food.

The present Mir, a light-skinned man with sleek, jet-black hair and a prominent nose, wears a pink Ralph Lauren polo shirt and introduces his wife, the *Rani*. She is a vibrant, sophisticated Indian from Bombay who shows she is a New Age Woman by occasionally contradicting him.

Mirshab (as he is referred to in his kingdom) explains the land ownership system whereby Hunzakuts never sell to outsiders. A woman can own property only when there is no son. The new generation doesn't want to farm, he says. "We need a college up here next year." Other plans include an extended runway for Boeing aircraft and a world class hotel with a disco and imported management.

At the Mir's palace, the plumbing is uncertain, but the apricot soup offered as a dessert is glorious; and the sight of Mt. Rakaposhi, at 25,000 feet, rising from behind his garden, would be a great sight anywhere. For me, the high point of my visit to Hunza was the evening Call to Prayers.

It was twilight. I was washing up for dinner and stepped outside to sniff the night and see if I needed a wrap, when — attracted to a movement just above me — I realized there was something, animal or human, up there.

In the almost-dark, at treetop level, a man with his head wrapped in a turban was climbing up on the palace roof, balancing himself, paper-thin, straight and tall. Across the river that separates Hunza from its old enemy, Nagar, he stood still and called

Transparency — a Pakistan street.

out to the faithful. His cry bounced back to us, and the voices of other callers echoed from the mountains on the other side, hanging suspended over the valley. The sky darkened and the first stars appeared until — much too soon — his harmonious rounds faded out, and I was left sitting on the grass, just the silhouette of the mountains visible now, looking, hearing, wondering, in a penetrating silence.

Back at the family inn, we hear more about Chitral Province from Judy, a newcomer who appears at the long table for supper. She is a nurse-practitioner with Freedom Medicine, which trains Afghan men to be paramedics and has just signed on for her second year, receiving room and board and $500 a month.

"What is the quality of life," we ask, "for the women you see?"

"They are all Suni Moslem, in tight *purdah*," she says. "Only a few come to the clinic, hidden behind their *burquas*."

"They can see only a female doctor?"

"It's up to the man in charge of them. They do not come in alone. Mostly, they have their babies at home with family midwives; they only come when there are complications. Last winter, when only our male doctor was on duty here, there was a woman brought in by her father. She needed a Cesarean section and, at first, he agreed; later, he revoked his permission."

"What happened?"

"The baby died."

Many things we saw and heard in the Chitral area pointed to the lack of human rights that we, as Americans, take for granted. As we moved westward through the Gilgit river valleys, however, much that we saw, heard and felt seemed touched by a pastoral purity. We kept our cameras ready; the images had a morning-dew freshness about them.

The thought of crossing what the British called "The Northwest Frontier," from east to west was initiated by a Swiss walking buddy, whom I had originally met in India and kept up with by mail. She was enamored with Pakistan because it was still so "untouched." Hearing of my plans to travel there, she wrote me "If you feel brave enough, you can try to get a jeep and go on the rough journey over the Shandur Pass." I carry this letter in my pocket as Jane and I start out from Hunza.

Once we leave the paved road, two hours out, we cross a raw land of few people and marginal farms. We are slowed by cows, and at low points, by water over our hubcaps. As winter is approaching, we see families returning from higher ground to the their homes in the three valleys we cross: Ishkoman; Yasin; and Ghizer. A young father carries a baby while the women lead donkeys whose backs are laden with cut peat. Soon, they will be snowed in for six months. Now they are as bedazzled by us as we are by them.

"What ARE you doing here?" a schoolboy, practicing his English, asks as he finds us trudging through his valley, on an impromptu stroll we take as we wait for Gophar to change a tire. In his village, we watch windblown women in flowered dresses, sifting grain. No other outsiders are here except for a British medical unit, inoculating babies, whose faces are smeared with ashes to ward off the evil spirits, for smallpox and polio. We smile a lot, feeling the weight of being the only Americans these people may have ever seen.

We are at Phunder Lake now, far away from the tourist trade of Hunza with its needlepoint belts and pale pink Indian "rubies." We stay in lonely splendor at Government Rest Houses, another residue from colonial times, where a small staff unlocks doors, heats up cans of soup and indifferently maintains the premises, anticipating some political personage on an important mission.

Across tundra, we stop at a high checkpoint, where we get out of the jeep and sit on the rough ground, drinking tea from china cups with the border guards who are bored to death. They are delighted when Jane strikes up a jaunty Shandur Pass tune on a recently-acquired antique horn, the *surnay*.

We are on the kind of switchback road that has been obliterated in most of the USA; in places even our narrow wheelbase can't make the turn without backing up. At a certain point, we make a wizard's turn from north to east, and dead ahead of us is Tirich Mir, the highest mountain in the Hindu Kush, our touchstone for Chitral, another friendly kingdom of the past, where the river Oxus flows.

The gorge, from Mastuj on, is a devilish chameleon of fantastic shapes and colors. In the dark, we arrive at Chitral village, sprawled out at the meeting of two rivers. The lay of the land, the smell of dried grass, make me think of Montana or Idaho.

All visitors must register with the police here, and the Afghans have taken over. It's hard to tell who is a true *Mujaheddin* — fighter of the Holy War — as all the men appear in the Afghan-style turban, well-worn combat boots and carry the ubiquitous rifle on their shoulders.

When we go walking on the outskirts of town, we experience the Muslim code of hospitality, and can't go more than a few yards without being pulled into someone's courtyard. The customs that envelop their own women don't apply to us. Men come out of the fields to show off their baby sons and offer us their produce: pomegranates here, apples there. Sign language, cameras and music are the go-betweens. In one house, Parsi is the language; in another, Khowar. When Fida tells us there are 52 different Muslim sects, we begin to grasp the inevitability of tribal isolation — and the abstract nature, in such a country, of national laws.

The ambiance in Chitral town is faintly sinister. Women are absent, and the bazaar is a lush market where red plush and knives dominate. We sense fabrics aren't what's making the place run. It's drugs, we are told — "the best hashish in the world" — and guns sold on the back streets. Families, we hear and read, are going without food and clothes to assemble huge arsenals.

By now, we have given up trying to file our experiences away into comfortable niches. Most of what we see and feel lies outside of our previous experiences. There is a strict value system at work here, but it is not, for the most part, one we know. Culture shock thus becomes part of living in western Pakistan; and several decades after the British moved on, we understand why the word "frontier" has clung to the region.

We go through the gentle Lowari Pass and the towns of the Dir area, where the sound of guns being fired into the air dominate the market place. (The customer is "test-driving" before he buys.) The wild roads fall gradually behind us, and we begin to see cars that aren't jeeps. Overflowing buses hog the roads and lead us into Peshawar, the city that looks West and is both geographically and historically, linked to the Khyber Pass. Fida knows all westerners are curious about the Khyber and promises he will try to get us there.

We must write a letter, he tells us, "respectfully" asking permission. Then, we must go to three offices, one with records piled from floor to ceiling along one wall. Then we collect our "guard," an enormous farm boy with strong B.O. that wafts back to Jane and me in the back seat. It's an hour up to Landi Kotal where we get out and look over the bleak hills of Afghanistan. We are not encouraged to stop, possibly, we decide, to keep us from poking around.

The Pathan compounds are an attraction: mud forts with ten-foot walls and, on each of their four corners, turrets with gun slits.

"Government installations?" I ask.

"No! No! Houses. These people have enemies. They don't sleep at night!"

Last summer, we hear, there was a tribal war involving more than 10,000 people. But on this quiet morning, the road is disarmingly ordinary — with guileless signs of "Thank you! Thank you!" placed here and there along the way, suggesting drivers are on their way in or out of Yellowstone Park.

At Lahore, we are back in civilization in the two large rooms we take at another PTDC, Dean's Hotel, which has a liquor permit

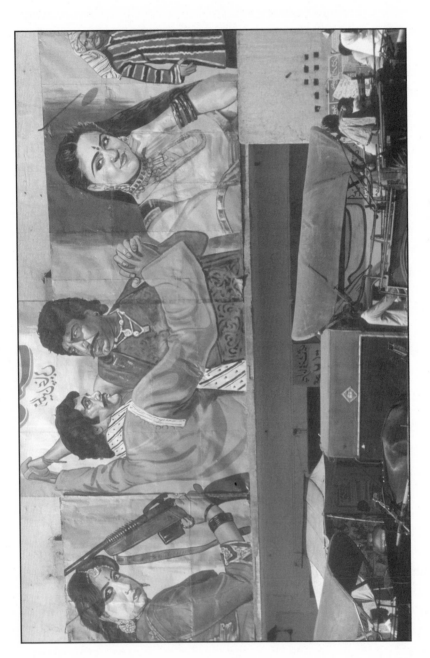

Movie posters and hansom cabs, street scene, Lahore.

room for the unholy. There, we write out our mother's maiden name and other pertinent bits of I.D., after which a man behind the bar passes over a bottle wrapped in brown paper.

We fall into a routine of having a gin and tonic with the 7:00 foreign news. Benezir Butto, the current Prime Minister, is on regularly. The controversial "daughter of the east" with a Radcliffe/Oxford education, she is a cool, beautiful enigma, as she tries to keep her *dupatta*/scarf from slipping off her head in a diplomatic juggling act. She has many factions to satisfy and, like the Pathans, many enemies.

Here, in the bazaars of the old walled city of Lahore, I have a few close encounters with women. They come to buy food and fabrics, usually with the veil over the head and poised to flip up over the nose (so that, then, only the eyes are revealed). I try to blend into the stalls, fix my lens and shoot fast, finding they will often allow me to catch them with my camera, especially if no man is around.

Once, on one of those market mornings — in an unnerving, but delightful gesture that replays for me over and over at its fullest intensity — a completely covered woman reaches out from behind her *burqua* and starts pumping my hand. I feel a strong flow of energy coming my way, woman to woman. I don't know exactly why because our words to each other are gibberish and ALL I can see of her is the blank, opaque curtain that covers her face, on top of the tent that hides her body.

On our last night at Dean's, Fida gets us invited to a wedding. Walking home in a soft twilight, we hear the music, see the lights, slip under a tent where the women of the bride's family are dancing to sitars and drums. They sweep us in, make us eat, drink, surround us, hover, ask our names. Now we are strewn with wreaths of marigolds; now they are touching our hair. We fall back in our chairs, dizzy with the visual overkill of satins, lames, and silks in vibrating colors, on little girls, stunningly made up! Then the Mother of the Bride opens my palm and smacks me, hard, with a blop of something that I fear is cow dung, or worse, and makes me hold it tight — so the dye will take, I find out. It's henna, the good luck tattoo of the Muslim world.

We say good-bye to Gophar, who can't stop grinning because he's going home to his wife and children. Fida doesn't mention domesticity, but is happy to trundle off with his gift from Jane, her turquoise jacket he has coveted. His parting duty is to see us off on the bus back towards India, where the scene is the usual, muddy, bus-stop chaos. We have reserved seats, on the last row, and I am indignant that we have to sit in these bumpy seats, the dregs, for five hours. I start to object when something in Fida's face makes me pause. Jane says, "I wouldn't do that."

I look again and notice that ALL the women are in the back. That's where the women sit — over the springs.

Underway, in the late afternoon light that falls across the empty Punjab, I catch another image that stays with me: a turbaned man, all in white, isolated in the desert. He sits cross-legged on a blanket, under a makeshift canopy propped up with three sticks. An odd sunbeam spotlights him as our bus drives past, while he sews away, benignly, improbably — unforgettably — on a black Singer sewing machine.

I take a deep breath, put my head back on the jarring seat, close my eyes, pull my fist in tight over my henna, and try to hang onto the memory of my strange Pakistan blessings.

Along the way, I discover "Real Travel", as opposed to the kind that's cooked up by a hotel chain. RT entails a movement of consciousness, as well as of feet. Flexibility – and humility, for that matter – are necessary. In time, I write out a few guidelines that helped me stay on track.

RULES FOR REAL TRAVEL

1. Go to a different culture.
2. Go alone.
3. Go simply (luxury isolates & insulates).
4. Go lightly (one suitcase or pack you can carry).
5. Go without an itinerary.
6. Speak the language, even if you don't know how.
7. Don't rent a car unless you have to.
8. Dress ethnic and eat ethnic.
9. Look for connections, not differences.
10. Leave your assumptions behind.

Note: Rules 2 & 4, put you in control.
The rest are various ways you choose to give it up.

9   The Unpaved Road:

Guatemala

Nothing zaps up the adrenaline like uncertainty. It was morning and I was in Bacalar in the southeastern Yucatan. As I prepared to leave my pretty lakeside hotel, stuffing my thief-proof purse with four separate zippered compartments down my bosom, trying to memorize some phrasebook Spanish, I sat expectantly on the curb waiting for the bus. After fifteen minutes, a Mexican woman on her way to work asked me in Spanish where I was trying to go. When I said, "Chetumal," she signaled me with signs and more words I didn't know, to follow her out to the main road, Route 30. There, she indicated, was the bus stop. I was so over anxious that I had been waiting in the driveway of the hotel.

For the solo traveler off the beaten track, false starts are as normal as missed meals and lumpy beds. My miscue en route to Chetumal was merely one of many acceptable bumps on the road I traveled along the coast of Quintana Roo, into neighboring Belize and onward, I hoped, to Tikal.

Everything I had read about Tikal, the great ceremonial center of the ancient Mayan civilization, made me want to go there. And not by the tiny plane most visitors take to the excavated ruins in the jungles of northeastern Guatemala, but by the only road that connects it with the outside world, the road I had "found" on my map. The essence of my journey was to be self-discovery. The last thing I wanted was the quick and easy.

I'd been in limbo for a year, derailed on the Nanny track, fulfilling the prescribed role of one who has just celebrated her seventieth birthday. It was a glorious party: flowers, toasts — my life story in rhyme and song, beginning to blur into myth. I was previewing my own funeral, and, in some cobwebby corner, I KNEW this was not all I wanted in the final lifeplan. My Wake Up Call came as I lifted my grandson up to help me blow out the candles. As our breathing dovetailed, I felt my life sliding out from under me.

I had to get my hands out of the diaper bag and get back to the particular kind of moving around the world that I had done for fifteen years. It invited disturbances and the reshuffling of one's assurances. It was the open classroom, breathing OUT, learning to think differently. I was dismayed at how many computers there were in my community, but how few were used to think globally. The potentials of the internet revolution for increasing human understanding had been barely addressed, nor had travel as a fruitful way to read the foreign mind.

Now, after bus hops to Chetumal and Belize City, I had climbed aboard my dream bus on the long road to Tikal. I had heard rumors, false I was sure, that this was the *Bandito* Road.

The way is disarmingly straight, the people here a mix of African and Caribbean peoples, speaking English. Out of nowhere, dramatic mountains rise up ahead. "Guatemala!" I imagine, but learn later these are the Mountain Pine Ridges of Western Belize.

The bus is scattered with European backpackers discussing where we will be at nightfall. Two have bought tickets to the Guatemalan bordertown of Benque Viejo. My guide book advises "cross early in the morning — best chance of catching buses onward." I opt to get off the bus at the last town in Belize, San Ignacio, where there will be a choice of hotels.

Next morning, I find myself on a back road in the Cayo country where horses run free in a field as I wait for a school bus. It drops me off at the Guatemalan border, a scene of misinformation and confusion. But, once the customs formalities are over, I am persuaded to share a group taxi and find myself, effortlessly, in a comfy vehicle on the way to the place on the map where the bus heads north to Flores and on to Tikal. I am thoroughly enjoying myself, talking photography with a biologist from Berlin, when — flashing past me on the left side of the road — I am astonished to see a huge poster of a Comic Strip bandit facing me. He has a facemask; a twirling mustache; and two pistols pointing at everything that goes down the road. Above him, in oversized lettering, the warning: *"Peligroso!* (Danger!) *Banditos!"*

How can this be? We ARE on the bandito road! No turning back now.

"I've got on my Guatemalan shirt," I say bravely. "If they come on board, they won't attack ME!"

"Shhhh!" says the Berliner in my ear, as if the masked men were nearby. There aren't even any bushes outside for them to hide in, or any hills. The land is flat, treeless and empty.

As the taxi drops us off at the Main Parking lot of the Tikal National Park, I'm thinking, "Home Free!" — flushed with the sense of accomplishment that only the small-time risk-taker knows. It wasn't so hard on my road, after all. It was fun! I would stay for two, maybe three nights, right here where I could walk into the jungle at any hour — really SEE this wonderful place. I was ready for a few services. Which hotel? There were three. I picked the simplest with the most rooms, the Jungle Lodge.

As I went up to the desk, it was still only lunch time. "We're completely full," they said.

"Full? I thought it was the slow season."

I was suspicious. Maybe they didn't want to bother with one person. I wasn't part of a Conspicuous Consumption Group, buyers, eaters, drinkers, with dollar signs on their foreheads.

"O.K. I'll go to The Jaguar Inn."

"That's full too."

"The Tikal Inn?"

"They have no rooms, I just called over there."

No one to blame but myself, and I was furious! Of course it didn't matter that there were few tourists in the rest of Mexico, everyone in the world wanted to see the great Tikal.

"O.K. what are my options?"

"I'm sure you can find a room at Flores. There's a shuttle bus at 2:00 or you can see the ruins this afternoon and go back later."

"I just CAME from Flores," I moaned, "and that's not where I want to be. I want to be at Tikal. I've spent two days traveling to get here."

("Real travelers never go back!" I murmured, *sotto voce*.)

Then I remembered something. "There's a campground here, isn't there? You have hammocks for rent?"

It was her turn to be surprised. "Yes," she said, "you can rent a hammock."

When I inspected the campgrounds, I found a wide green lawn, about 20 concrete platforms, spread far apart — the toilets close by with a guard outside. I knew about hammocks. I'd stayed on the beach in one on the coast just north of here, only five days ago.

I was shown to a platform already occupied by Marcella, from Costa Rica, twenty-one, dark-eyed and wispy in a long graceful skirt, and Lili, a cool, leggy blond in denim shorts from Denmark. They had a camp stove and sleeping bags. All the young men who worked on the grounds hovered around with matches and wood, wanting to be near them because they were both artlessly gorgeous: the light and the dark beauties — who seemed not to know how they dazzled. Tonight, inside the ruins at their favorite site, *El Mundo Perdido*, (The Lost World), they were having a tiny celebration of Lili's 18th birthday — candles and cake at 6:00, if I wanted to come along.

The day seemed to go on forever. At four I went by myself into the vast ruins set in a 575 square kilometer preserve, right off the innocent graveled parking lot, past a guard who collected $3, to find myself suddenly enveloped by jungle. The path was narrow and rough with exposed roots crawling underfoot; the trees went straight up, up, up on either side, and as I walked in a long way, it got darker and denser and the birds began to screech. Still with no ruins in sight, I realized a howler monkey was swinging through the branches over my head. For the first time since I left home, I longed for company on the unpaved road. I worried about birds eyeing my white hair for nesting material (I'd had a run-in with an Oyster Catcher in the Hebrides years ago!); it crossed my mind that a python could be up among the monkeys. I'd watched NOVA.

At last I came around a corner and there, facing me across a wide open space, was the pyramid like no other: the Giant Jaguar, 44 meters high. Ah-Cacau's son, succeeding to the throne in 734, the stelae tell us, left his father buried with jade and pearls under the Giant jaguar. The sense of power is still present.

Standing before it, I found myself stretching to be taller, like a very small child before some influential uncle whose approval I sought. (I could feel him touch my shoulder and say: "Straighten up!") The building, a piece of architecture, itself had life. It stopped me in my tracks and held me.

After this first encounter, I wandered on several miles, finding other landmarks, sometimes following my guidebook, sometimes getting lost. As the afternoon waned, I encountered a British group, studying birds. They had their scope on an orange-breasted falcon — way up with the sun full on its improbable vest. Coming across others talking along the trails, I noticed that I was having trouble hearing.

"What?" I kept asking.

It was the birds taking over the ruins. They were all one could hear. As this mild Spring night came on, it was if the jungle was reasserting its superiority. Way up high, where I couldn't see them, the voices of tropical birds was deafening. I caught flashes of their bright long tail-feathers. They were courting, arguing, pulling down vines.

I was losing my light. Having no flashlight, I wouldn't be able to get myself home if I stopped for the birthday party. So walking faster and faster, the eyes of bird, monkey and snake following me, at last I reached the parking lot, in the dark.

From here, I had to find my concrete slab among all the other platforms on the campground. I started out blindly across the dark expanse of field. There were holes here and there and the grass was wet. There were a few scattered lights, but I didn't want to barge into someone else's bedroom. My beauties, I guessed, were still in the jungle, eating cake.

As I kept walking, however, I noticed one light set lower than the others. I headed for it and it began to look as if it was in the right place. Closer still, I saw it was sitting on the concrete slab. I saw my hammock and my suitcase. My beauties had been thinking ahead. They had set a tiny votive candle out for our way home. What a relief! Home free one more time.

But I was wrong again. The night air in Mexico and Belize had been so warm that I did not foresee the cold that fell over me as I lay down in that denim hammock on the edge of the Tikal jungle. As the night crept onward, I gradually emptied my suitcase, putting on layers, wrapping my head in a towel, wrapping myself entirely in the denim so that only my breath leaked out. Still, I was too freezing to cross the grass again to ask for a blanket, and, when I heard the beauties' return after midnight, too chagrined at my lack of preparedness, to ask them for help.

I was getting what I asked for, no frills, spontaneous, be-your-own-leader stuff. Disturbances were daily and the agony/ecstasy factor was high.

On the morning after my night in the campgrounds, I had had enough of hammocks, but I wanted to see more of Guatemala. I left Tikal from Flores, in a plane that lifted over a densely-covered, terrain of rounded hills as far as the eye could see. Each one could be hiding another Giant Jaguar. Sitting just behind the cockpit, I could see the two pilots peering up at a torn map they had scotch-taped above their control panel. It was just an hour onto the band-aid airstrip of Guatemala City, a sprawling, polluted place of over a million inhabitants and the takeoff hub to the Guatemalan "highlands."

For the next few days, I followed a popular route through the highlands — first to Antigua, then to Lake Atitlan and the villages around the lake. As a physical setting, this area blasts the senses. Walking through Antigua, the late afternoon light falls on its vividly painted walls, and a stranger orients herself by noticing whether the volcano *Aqua* (water) or *Fuego* (Fire) rises from the end of the cobblestone street.

I teamed up with Jan, a photographer from L.A., to climb by bus up to Chichicastinango (6800 ft.) for the fabled market there. We arrived at mid-day at this huge-scale photo-op. *Gringos* from all over the world aim their cameras and Camcorders at the Indians, mostly women and children who try to hide their faces without actually leaving the scene, as they also need to go home that day with money in their pockets. One part of me was uncomfortable to be lined up with all the other exploiters in such a World Class tourist trap, trying to sneak pictures for my own use; another part was caught up in the obvious, palpable magic element that was there, the quality the Spanish embody in the word, *maravilloso*. In this twice-a-week market, there was something above the ordinary. It was both a commercial and a religious event (not unlike the Indian Pushkar Fair).

As soon as you get off the bus, everything leads to the steps of the church of Santo Tomas. Pushed along by a squash of bodies, you play follow the leader to a scene of ordered chaos. The white towers of the church rise behind a foreground jammed with cala lillies, iris, fruit and native women covered in vibrant textiles. Just outside the church doors, in front of lighted candles and offerings of flowers, several Indian men and women are swinging incense pots so energetically across the threshold that they appear and disappear in the clouds of smoke.

Sunday market, threshold of Santo Tomas, Chichi.

And the smell! The previous night, in a restaurant in Antigua, I had met Kirsten, an American who told me she was studying Mayan ethnobotany, writing a doctoral thesis on the plant from which the Indians derive their incense. "Obscurity Central!" was my first reaction. Now I saw it differently. This strong, pungent, knock-you-over aroma, could not be from any old leaf in the forest. The last time I'd smelled anything like it was in front of the Jokhang temple in Lhasa. I wasn't surprised to learn later that the purpose of this part of the Sunday Market offering at Chici, whose origins are ancient, is to ask the spirits who guard the church for pardon for trespassing. The intensity on the faces of the swinging cloud makers told me they did not feel they were alone on those steps.

Jan and I had two perfect days of sightseeing around Lake Atitlan in a motor boat launch named "Betty" whose interior was painted turquoise. We bounced over the water to the village of Santiago Atitlan where the streets are lined with curtains of textiles. A clan of women — Tzutuhil Mayans — sit in the family display booths, each trying to persuade you to buy the piece with "her" bird or "her" frog. I was indifferent to the subject of *huiples*/embroidery until I spent an hour walking their streets and visiting their courtyards where they work outside on backstrap looms and invite the passerby in to see their work. Santiago had the feel of a working village, men going about their business, hitching rides in boats identical to ours, carrying machetes to work. As at the Chichi market, it possessed the sense of a place which, for economic survival, had opened its doors to outsiders, but had not yet been transformed by them.

Like much that goes on in a foreign country, it is sometimes possible to decode the babble, to get the drift of the bird-talk, but, in Central America, without the details contained in the language, I was finding that most encounters were a series of frustrations.

As with the frosty night that fell down on me at Tikal, I was caught unaware. This was different than Asia, where the lasting imprint of the British had left English as the language of commerce and of the educated. Here the visitor was cut out of a vastly rich and complex tangle of threads, a great ball whose core was embedded in the history, literature and art of Spain which had blended with the culture of its indigenous people.

I was stuck on the other side of the T-shirt I had seen in the international Visa Card office in Guatemala City: "English is spoken here, but not understood." If I managed to ask the question, I couldn't understand the Spanish answer. Most questions were too hard. I could only ask ones that began with "What?" "Where?" and "Who?" I wanted to ask "How?" and "Why?

The reflections in the lake — the pink dawn outlining the cones of volcanoes — were distant postcards. After a while, their shallowness mimicked the thinness my "Real Travel" had become. Two weeks before the departure date on my return flight, I decided the best thing I could do with the time left was to stop moving and deep-dive into one of Antigua's renowned Spanish schools. With the advantage of the Long Count of the Mayan calendar, it might not be too late to learn the verb declensions of a new language.

After that, my day began and ended with Juan Castillo's face. I can still hear his pure voice, the dark eyes holding mine fixedly as he repeated, and repeated again, the right way to say the words. I would try to block my linear thinking and just hear the cadence. That way I could SOMETIMES imitate what he had said. We sat in an open-air, bamboo-enclosed cubicle, about four feet square, set in a grassy lawn behind the colonial house which was the office of the school. This was one of about 35 schools in Antigua, the 5,000 foot high town, once the capital of New Spain and strewn with churches, monasteries and picturesque ruins rearranged by frequent earthquakes.

Right away, I loved the one-to-one format of "total immersion." Exiled just days ago from the language, now the language was all there was. No English was tolerated in class, and none was allowed, or understood, in my new home.

I lived now at Dona Estella's. A block and a half away from the school, through a high double wooden door, for which I had a key, I came and went as I pleased — and this Guatemalan *mestizo*, born the year after me, her husband who did not work, her children and grandchildren, and Consuelo, the maid, became my family. The bathroom, with hot water, was on the first floor and my bedroom was on the second, along with Claudia's, a German student and Jane's, an English student, both the age of my daughters. I had a thin mattress with heavy blankets, a chest of drawers, a mirror, a desk, a light and a door with a padlock, but I had no window. At night I propped my door open to catch the air and I slept well in spite of banging pipes, washing that began in the dark and church bells at 5:00 AM. Everything was very clean, the food was indifferent, and the price was $160 a week, for room and board, and four hours of one-to-one language classes.

I did not have time to want anything else. My day was complete with lessons, homework, and new friends of all ages, from every country, all studying Spanish at various levels. Though I was relieved not to be going anywhere, I was reciting *voy, vas, va, vamos, van* (the verb "to go") in my sleep, until even the interior advice I gave myself was sprinkled with Spanish.

After a week, I tried to extend my plane ticket, and when I could not, I felt cheated. On my last day in Antigua, I took off for school with my bag packed so I could fit in a morning break with Juan who wanted to show me his favorite church, the Iglesia de San Francisco. A lovely place, the interior walls lined with messages of *gracias* to its resident father, Hermano Pedro, who founded a hospital there in the 1600s and is now up for sainthood: thanks for getting someone a job, thanks for making someone well. The oldest ones are engraved into marble, the newest scrawled on file cards.

I told Juan I believed in scientific medicine, not in the kind of miracles where you said a prayer and threw away your crutches. He said, resignedly, his brown eyes, sad, and looking right at me: "I know." On our coffee break yesterday, he had already told me he had no wish to go to America. He did not think there was any tradition and religion there.

End of the line, Chichicastenango.

On those unpaved roads deep in the southern hemisphere, I was, for five weeks, often in the dark, lost — and wrong. But I was "someplace else." Swaying on the overhead straps, sometimes the only outsider on the bus, I looked out at an unfamiliar, changing scene every mile along the way. I felt ageless — a work as in flux as the chameleon hanging on the edge of the screen.

I'm not sure how to name what I brought back, from either the classroom or the rest, but all of the travel I had done verified, over and over, that life is full of many mysteries. In the land where the marvelous, without ceremony, is kneaded into the corn-flour, I like to imagine that some of the lumps cleared customs and came home with me.

III. Mavericks

Contrarily, just as I've become an advocate for solo travel, I feel lucky to secure a place on a "Peace Walk" in the Ukraine organized by Political Science students at Georgetown (D.C.) It's the summer of 1988 when the way most tourists get into Russia is on the In-Tourist itinerary, widely reviewed as overpriced, contrived and tedious.

Six years later, in 1994, another lucky break comes along when a magazine editor invites me on a Press Trip to Normandy. The article that emerges, "Voices From a Far Shore," is another improbable maverick that breaks all my own rules, but is much too rich a story to leave out.

No two visits abroad delivered more insights. If I know anything about what it is to be a Norman, or a Ukrainian, it is because of these two inspired undertakings that don't fit into the "Real Travel" mold.

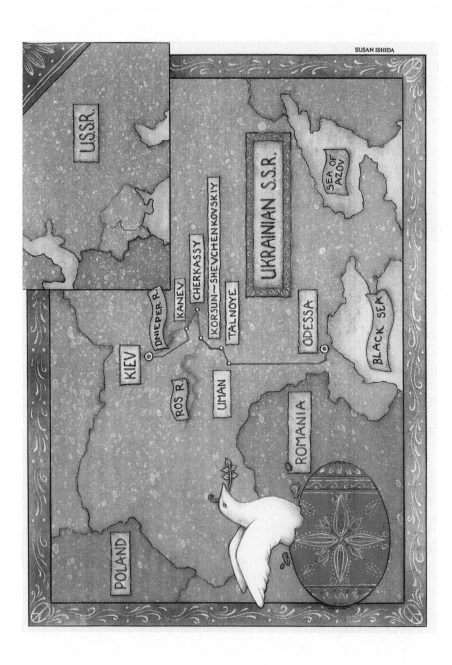

10   Slit in the Iron Curtain:

Peace Walk, Ukraine, 1988

The rain woke me at 5:00 AM. On my roof of taut, rip-stop nylon, the sound was soothing. Soon it would be dawn and a long line of scruffy campmates would queue up in front of the unisex privies. Hoping to avoid this humiliation, I put on my raincoat, unzipped the rain-flap of my tent, crept out into the dark and started looking for my own private corner of the athletic field. Erratic snores welled up from the ground inside other plastic domes, warning me of tent-lines stretched at ankle height, just right for tripping. I moved out of the camp's hub to the encircling path and, just as my eyes adjusted to the dripping density, I realized someone was watching me.

Backed up against the ten-foot cyclone and barbed-wire fence, was a heavy man crouched under a large umbrella. He was looking straight at me, but pretending not to see: a blind starer. It was a tense moment before my shuddering stopped and I figured out he was a security guard on the graveyard shift. For the first time since our plane landed two days before, I knew I was in the Soviet Union.

Prejudice is part of the luggage an American carries with her as she descends the ramp of her Aeroflot plane. I knew how it would be — from old newsreels, John le Carre thrillers and Secre-

taries of Defense speeches. I knew what to expect because I had
just been through an "indoctrination" in Washington, D.C.

The thrust of our lessons was "They are NOT like us!" Soviets think collectively, the experts told us, and have a strong aversion to risk-taking. "The nail that sticks up gets hammered!" is
what Russian mothers tell their children.

The purpose of our trip was not pleasure, our leaders warned,
but to act as "Citizens Diplomats," although few of us then understood what the job description called for. Through a slit in the Iron
Curtain, we and our Soviet counterparts were going to promote trust
and friendship between our two countries. We were going to encourage the thaw in the Cold War and learn for ourselves about each other.
Some of us thought of our adventure as a strenuous experiment in
international living or a way to go to Russia in a time when the canned
trips run by the Soviet tourist bureau were all that were available.
Others were global thinkers with long-range dreams of one day replacing force with cultural interaction.

We all attached ourselves to an unwieldy microcosm of over
500 men and women. Half Soviet, half American, with a few
(nuclear free) New Zealanders participating. We had agreed to
travel together some 400 miles from Odessa to Kiev, much of it on
foot, through the villages of the Ukraine where most of the townspeople had never seen an American. We were a bilingual camp
that bused, walked, ate, talked, worked and played together for
28 days in August/September of 1988, moving with our giant appendages on an almost daily basis.

American participants were self-selected, came from twenty-seven states and paid their own way. Soviets were chosen; their
government paid. About a third came from the Moscow area, a
third from the Ukraine and another third represented the other
republics of the USSR. Average age was probably 35; in general,
the Soviets seemed to be an older assortment. I was an elder of
the "Over-50" group of about that many Americans who never
stopped giving advice.

We were 35 hours en route, going by the northern route from the West coast via Seattle, and arrived in Moscow at midnight where we were whisked through Customs and transferred to a smaller plane to Odessa. Around 2:00 AM, we walked out into the gentle air across a dimly-lit runway soaked with rain. As we peered out into the dark, someone said, "There are people over there, way behind the fence." "Lots of people!" a raised voice echoed. One by one, as if we were all moving in slow motion, we became aware that they were waiting for us. A long stretch of glistening asphalt space still separated us, and we waited uncertainly. Then a young American walker — blond, fit, mod in his crushed denim and Mohawk haircut — put down his skateboard and started snaking across the space between us. A few of us started moving out behind him, then more, and more, and more, faster and faster — til in a great surge, we met in the middle, helter-skelter, like so many stalled Dodge'em cars.

I was alone as I crossed, and visibility was low. The first body I bumped up against was a man who kissed me on both cheeks. A woman appeared from behind him and pumped my hand vigorously. I managed to pronounce *dubree vaycher*/good-evening, and an impossible barrage of Cyrillic sound came back at me. A woman with red ribbons and crowns of flowers twined through her golden braids held out a mammoth loaf of decorated egg-bread with a tiny saucer of salt set in the middle of the loaf. "Eat! Eat!" she commanded in a deep, strong voice, showing me how to pull off a hunk and dip it in the salt. In the Soviet Union you only break bread with your friends, never your enemy.

Our 16 campsites were all different, yet they were all the same. Because we were a horde of over 500, we often camped "in the middle of nowhere," our tent-cities on the grounds of pioneer youth Camps, vocational schools or Recreation Centers, sometimes using their abandoned buildings of unlovely, deteriorating ferro-cement. Far preferable to this, were the close-in sites on village greens or local parks. We camped on the Black Sea, on a beach in the territory of Ros, on a river near the Korsun-Shevchenkousky border, on the polluted Dneiper.

We bused 20 miles out into the country for our second site — the gate, the fence, tables, benches, everything in the entire "camp" — had been constructed for our one-night stay.

Wherever our caravansary went, teeth-brushing, shaving and washing were performed in front of plastic basins, 20 attached in a long row, mirror in front, soap and towel at the side. On the back of this contraption hung a five-gallon container, kept full by a stout matron in white who carried buckets from the water truck that followed us. The Ukrainians built dozens of outhouses for us — the paint often tacky, the wood raw. Curtains, wherever they appeared were pristine, just put up. Portable showers went with us and offered hot water at specified hours. Colorful, striped tents housed this glory where, on the female side, ten naked women were under the always-on water and twenty more lined up in the steam, trying to keep their towels dry. Our shower was a great socializing agent. I can still conjure up certain women, from both countries, as I first connected with them in the swarming mist of overlapping bodies. When Tanya wordlessly passed over her shampoo as mine ran out, I did not forget her face.

As I sank into my Thermarest, the last late murmurs from the camp were always rich in the new language I was trying to learn. Every meeting, every meal and bus ride was a struggle to cross the language barrier. Phrase books out in front of us, we tried to ask each other questions, clutching onto the bilingual among us — our Ambassadors, most of them Soviets, and, we heard, chosen for this facility.

We talked about Afghanistan, where the Russians were mired down and Vietnam, where the US had a parallel experience. We discussed religion, alcohol, rent, health care, child care, nuclear build-up, abortion, male chauvinism, consumer goods, freedom of speech, freedom to travel, music, education, defectors, prejudice, sports — and often the bottom line led to economics. There were no forbidden subjects, and we found that, while the Soviets were not "just like us," one of the glaring attributes we had in common was our ignorance of each other.

We were a portable city and did not travel light. Aside from the 13 buses that transported us when we weren't walking, we were followed by an entourage that included the vital catering truck, the laundry truck (three-day service), the medical facility (great, but if you went to the hospital with pneumonia, you endured "cupping"), and the repair truck, whose biggest business was in cameras and zippers. By the time we left Odessa, Alcoholics Anon. was meeting daily, Overeaters Anon., weekly, and a Stress workshop was in place for those people having trouble adjusting to living with 500 people. The heart of our dragon was the Sound truck, which dispensed Ukrainian, Russian and Western music; the schedule for the day, and sometimes stern censure, such as "Yesterday we were an hour late leaving camp!" It also yelled out announcements of impromptu events, like the arrival of the Ukrainian teachers. They had driven all day in a beat-up van to catch up with us, bringing books, games, and messages from their students. Our USA teachers were prepared and dug into their duffels to offer all kinds of classroom aids from the Capitalist world. The boisterous exchange, lasting far into the night, was one more activity that brought us together.

But walking provided the strongest glue.

Walking is the way a serious traveler moves. It sets him down in the midst of the action, homelander and visitor, eye to eye. In this case, it was the perfect icebreaker, and everyone knew how to do it. We all learned how to stride into the line of march and fall into step with someone. Each would peer at the other's Dog-Tag, trying to pronounce the foreign name. Soviet women pushed in close beside other women, and assertive Soviet men liked to lock their upper arm around yours, holding tight, moving out fast. We started off together, lining up around 10:00 AM behind the flags. A Soviet carried the Stars and Stripes, an American the Hammer and Sickle; and we took turns carrying the flag of the United Nations and the horizontal banner that read "American Soviet Walk."

The Soviets were usually destination oriented, while the Americans showed every form of deviation, becoming strollers, peeping through gates, talking to farmers about their potato crops. Jane was a Pied Piper, collecting children as she pulled trinkets from her bottomless sack. Bill confided to the USSR World War II vets that he, too, was a veteran — of the European theater — and came home with a remarkable series of photos of upright elders, their chests heavy with medals. Stragglers were picked up by the buses and deposited just off the town square, so we could all converge for the daily reception and speeches near the ubiquitous statue of Lenin near the town square.

The countryside looked strangely familiar, like the landscape of an old European movie, set in the early forties. It was flat and covered with tomato fields, corn, pear orchards and sunflowers — like Iowa. On the main highway between Odessa and Kiev, the authorities blocked off one side so we could walk on the road. Truck drivers leaned out of their cabs and waved to us; one family stopped their car on the closed side and raced across to give us two quarts of warm milk from their cow. Crowds filled the overpasses and jammed the crossroads. Wherever we went, school was out.

One-story cottages, newly painted, lined the narrow lanes of the villages. Blue is the color I remember and a gate with an outline of two swans. The family stood together, watching us go by — some faces closed wondering. Other locals cut flowers from their front gardens and, gold teeth glittering, rushed into the streets to thrust them into our arms.

Glasnost!! was the unprogramed ingredient in the contrived main events, its elements in the sound of the word: the eruption of the shell as the chicken bursts out of the egg — "the revolution without a shot." Glasnost was palpable and ingenuous. For me, it was epitomized by the farmer near Uman who leapt from behind a crowd of people I had stopped to shake hands with me on the road and swept me up in a crushing hug that I can still feel.

We walked, we talked, we listened, and then we stopped to eat — in style. The Ukrainians' forte was the romantic al fresco meal set between a row of poplars, backed by strolling musicians in folk costumes. Sultans' tents would be lined up on the side, in case of bad weather. Fabric, not paper; glass and metal, not plastic, were on the tables. Samovars, brimming with coffee and tea were in the corner, their looping silver/brass handles decorated with garlands of bread rings. Our standard breakfast was cucumbers, tomatoes, green peppers, green onions, served au naturel; beets, carrots and cabbage, lightly pickled; sausages galore, and many breads. At lunch, the biggest meal, beef stews, fish dishes, tasty soups, *pelmeni* meat dumplings and eggplant might be added to the fare. Supper was a lighter version of lunch. There was plenty of fruit, very little seasoning, no sauces — and fast service.

Despite the large number of security guards and rumored KGB (it was said their shoes gave them away), we had few restrictions, and the long summer days were full of unrehearsed scenes.

"Two-hundred-fifty Americans!? *Gdyeh? Gdyeh?*/Where? Where?"

Serge — who was pushing a toddler in a stroller and trailed by his wife, his wife's sister and his first-grader — was incredulous as he followed me into camp.

"Here! Look! Americans!" I pointed out when we got there. "Over there, Soviets!"

The Soviets, playing cards on the grass, looked up and said, reassuringly, "Yes! Yes! It's O.K."

I found Joe, one of our handful of staff who spoke Russian. He invited us all to sit on his tarp and talk. It evolved that Serge was a chemical engineer, desperately seeking news of the United States. Two hours later, he finally pulled himself away, his family still tagging along.

"We hear only propaganda," he told us "— Radio Moscow."

At another moment, Phil was kidnapped by an old man who drew him into his parlor to sample his best cognac. That was the day I decided to take a picture of a *babushka* who was coming out of her house which was set back among the trees along our route. From about 125 feet, I fixed my lens on her face, and as she came closer, I could see that she was crying, uncontrollably. I felt intrusive, but saw that she was trying to reach me — bent, leaning on her cane, inching forward with what I finally saw as we met was a crumpled clipping in her fist. Prying it from her, I saw a yellowed newspaper picture of Khrushchev and John F. Kennedy, meeting in 1961. She didn't want to give it to me, but to show it to me. She took both my hands in hers and tried to talk, but I didn't understand — exactly. Just after, Yuri, coming along behind me on the march, stopped to help.

"She wants to tell you she is happy to see the Americans come — after so long — in peace," he translated.

"*Mir e drushba*/peace and friendship," the old woman kept repeating.

I tried to learn these words. They seemed like the right words in this place where the war had left so many scars and seemed like yesterday.

Other scenes lost none of their charm by having been pre-planned. Valery, 38, the town dentist, and his wife Inge, 33, who has a part-time job at the school, had prepared weeks ahead to take three Americans, and the Soviet assigned to go with them into their home for the night. Off a side street of Yasnozorye village, we walked through a gate, into a big, grassy yard, to meet the grandfather who was taking the children off their hands for the occasion. We toured the three wooden cabins, saw the vegetable garden, the bee hives, the red car, heard of the extensive renovation they'd done on this property, which comes with his job.

The interior was crowded with possessions: they had a TV, but no phone and an archaic hot water system. The dining room was set for a banquet — for people, I thought afterwards, who remember being hungry. "Nothing on the shelves in the stores, but everything in the refrigerator," is a Ukrainian refrain, I was told. The feast was deftly served from a kitchen housed in a separate cabin. Afterwards, Valery sat in his socks, a boyish extrovert with brown eyes and a dimple.

"We need nothing from *perestroika*," he said, surprisingly. (This was the term for Gorbachev's attempt at economic restructuring.) "We have the black dirt, *chernozem*, the fresh air, nature. It's different in Moscow, where my cousin lives. Here, we go camping on holiday. I get half-salary when I retire. Why would we want more money?"

"You are a very lucky man with such a pretty wife," Jim teased, making Inge blush furiously, as we toasted her with their apple wine, agreeing.

To the Soviets, our Capitalistic money was tainted, but they wanted to know every detail of how rich we were. "How much do you make?" was ALWAYS the first question. Tall Jennie, from Los Angeles, told me a Russian had taught her to say, "It's not important to have a hundred rubles. What's important is to have a hundred friends." Friendship was another preoccupation. The second question was often, "How many friends do you have?"

The Soviet walkers clung together in a buddy system. Maria and Olga, both from Byelorussia, sat on the bus together, ate together and tented together; so did Alexel and Boris, both veterans of the The Great Patriotic War (WWII); so did Utegan and Askar, both Kazakhs. The Ukraine was, for many, we came to realize, a foreign country where Soviets from the other republics were uncertain of everything. Within the circle of friendship was support and safety.

On the banks of the meandering Ros River, 15 days on the road, I made a friend. Elena had high cheekbones and wore her blond hair in a French roll. She was an interpreter who was often called on when there was a sensitive point in the dialogue. I was thrilled when she chose to walk beside me and told me how she had learned English working for the Bolshoi Ballet in Leningrad, had shed an alcoholic husband and raised two daughters on her own. She exemplified the person who adheres to her own values, no matter what her government does. When the churches were closed, she told me, she never gave up practicing her religion. Reaching 55, however, Elena was forced into retirement.

"It was the worst year of my life! Suddenly, I was no one. I had no place, nothing to do. My phone never rang."

Then she heard of the proposed walk and was hired when she said the magic words: "I am fluent in English!" Yet the walk was a temporary solution; it would be over in two weeks. She was ready to step aside again and let youth have its chance.

"But you have experience, and judgment they don't have! You must fight for yourself!" I commanded — forgetting for a moment I was in a society where the idea of "self" had gone underground. Elena listened to me, the American who had been exactly in her place, learned how to be assertive and entered into the work field late in life. As we walked back from the river, we were no longer the American visitor and the Soviet interpreter. We were two women whose parallel stories had realigned us into kindred spirits. When it came time to give away my one and only bilingual T-shirt, it was Elena I gave it to.

As we lifted off for the long journey home, I put on my long-distance glasses and peered down at the vast, inert, blank territory below, an uneasy amalgam of old empires that stretched across 11 time zones. It seemed unlikely that 250 Americans on a 28 day walk could have affected it. Yet, even the most cynical among us, agreed that we had left an imprint. We had affected one another.

Over 250,000 Soviets had seen us in person, 100 million more through the media. We had done something together, on the same level, that wasn't always easy. We had exchanged more than toothpaste. Perhaps we had encouraged each other to be more fully human. John Mathers of Suitland, Maryland, one of the "Over 50" club, thought it might not be quite a first step, but, rather, "a shuffling of weight, a movement of our energies in a new direction."

11 Voices from A Far Shore:

Normandy Remembers, 1994

On a stormy day, when I could barely move against the wind, I walked among the stark white crosses of the American Cemetery and looked through the pine trees down onto Omaha Beach, pretending my tears were rain. My companion, Harry, who knew just how many young men had died on this five mile stretch 50 years ago, reached down and scooped a couple of red pebbles into his pocket. "Just right for Bloody Omaha," he murmured.

For years, we were told, propellers and parts of guns had washed up after storms, but little evidence is left on the shore of the fierce fighting that took place in the first hours of June 6, 1944. It could be any cold-water, pristine American beach now — Cape Hatteras or Point Reyes — an innocuous place scattered with gulls and seaweed.

In the Fall of 1993, I was here on assignment for a national magazine, anticipating the media opportunity of the fiftieth anniversary of the Allied Invasion and Liberation of Europe in World War II. The editors wanted impressions of the D-Day event from "the woman's perspective." Their readers, they guessed, had had their fill of battlefield memoirs.

The way to get another point of view, I thought, would be to talk to the civilian army of French women who had endured the

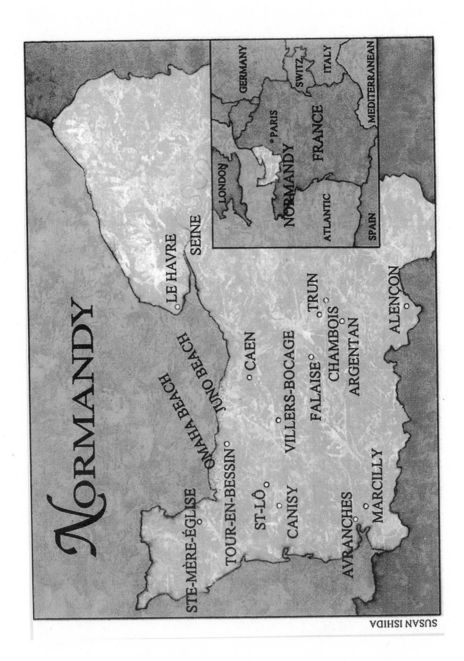

SUSAN ISHIDA

German occupation that lasted for over four years following the evacuation of their only allies, the British — pushed to the sea and dramatically evacuated by tiny boats from Dunkerque on June 3, 1940 — and the armistice signed by the French/Vichy government 19 days later. We certainly *had* heard from the soldiers, sailors and airmen of Eisenhower's Great Crusade, who eventually rescued them — but not from the families of France who received them.

This welcoming committee was made up of the women, the children and the men unfit to fight. Some of them had been working at home, underground, putting themselves in immense danger, to undermine the occupation and make way for the military advance.

As part of the generation who came of age in the 1940's, these women of Normandy were my other half. On the far shore, across the English Channel, it was they who met the men we said goodbye to. We were all untested and young, but unlike me, their initiations took place in the brutal arena of home warfare. The only hardship I knew was that all "the boys" had disappeared. The excitement in my life was reduced to USO dances, tracking planes for the Air Corps, and now and then receiving a censored V-Mail from a J.G. on a PT boat.

Through my magazine's connections in Normandy, I was able now, nearly 50 years later, to track down a few of these low-profile warriors who had been caught in the thick of the backyard action back then, enduring MUCH to smooth the path of the friendly "invaders" and contribute to the Allied victory.

In Caen, which saw so much heavy fighting, I was directed to Jacqueline Spoor who was 18 years old in 1944. She was still Jacqueline Neuville then and living with her parents in a large house that is now the Palace of Justice. In the four trying years of the German takeover, she and the rest of France had gotten used to restrictions: no heat in the schools ("Girls went in the morning, boys in the afternoon"); no radios ("but we listened in bed, anyway").

What Jacqueline remembers about the Allied invasion was the light: Just after midnight in Caen on June 6, "the sky was all white — you could read a paper by the light."

These were the parachutes and flashlights of the men of the British Sixth Airborne dropping down to secure the crossings over the River Orne.

"Later in the morning, in downtown Caen, everything looked normal, but a school friend whispered to me: 'You know, the English came.'"

The English — and the Americans, Canadians and French — had arrived with more planes, war ships, landing craft, guns and men than anyone had ever seen assembled in one assault in the history of the world. One hundred and fifty-six thousand men were put ashore in the first 24 hours after the Allied landings on the beaches, and it wasn't long before every family in northwestern France, each in its own way, was fighting beside them as they made their way inland and east to the Seine.

Seeking refuge from the heavy bombing of Caen, Jacqueline's father, a lawyer and Civil Servant, moved his family out, by bike and on foot, leaving everything behind. They went first to Villiers-Bocage, then on towards Trun. Unaware of which way the armies were moving, they wandered southeast, and found themselves caught in the path of the retreating Germans.

Jacqueline recalls an episode sometime in June when her father walked across a field to rejoin them and "bombs began falling on the road. He was on the battlefield!" Ultimately, as the Allies advanced on Chambois in mid-August, the family was swept along with the German Seventh Army who were escaping through the narrow passage between Falaise and Argentan. The fierce engagements fought in this sector proved to be the turning point in the battle of Normandy.

They had been running for two and a half months, when the ordeal ended. "At last," Madame Spoor told me, "we found perfect quiet, on a farm near Chambois. We entered the courtyard, and our hosts were grinning. They said, "We have some

Germans and Italians here who don't want to fight anymore! What shall we do with them?'" In an instant, the tension gave way, and "everybody — all of them — laughed!" The war, for them, was over.

A widow now, after 34 years of marriage to a British engineer who had landed June 7 on Juno beach in a *Canard* amphibious vehicle, Madame Spoor is a "don't look back" lady. Sixty-eight and blondish, she is carefully but simply put together in a way that is quintessentially French. Her current passion is Bridge. "I usually play 'til one in the morning," she admitted, "even if I'm losing."

While Madame Spoor remembered the light, Monique de Fallerans remembered the noise.

From her parents' Caen house on the wild, dark morning of June 6, Monique Leval, 21, heard "a terrible bombardment," and, on the ocean side, as dawn broke, "we saw a fine line of ships coming toward us." In the days that followed, the doors of her protected life gradually opened. German officers came to requisition a wing of the country house they fled to, and Monique began to meet Allied officers. Possibly trying to live up to her revered father, a much-decorated flyer, she was drawn into scouting for the Underground movement operating in Caen. On her first foray, in July 1944, she was caught, taken to Alencon 60 kilometers southeast and sentenced to death. But the German lieutenant in charge of her case granted a reprieve. "I've never killed women before and I don't want to start now," he told her. She was deported to a series of work camps, ending up at Ravensbruck near Berlin, where half of the camp inmates died before they were liberated.

Today Madame De Fallerans speaks with both eloquence and restraint about her ten-month ordeal of humiliation and deprivation. Her demanding mother, her controlled childhood, helped her, she told me. "It was," she said, "an education for survival."

When it was below freezing and her only dress was a flimsy cotton sheath, she told me, "I willed myself not to feel the cold."

An imposing woman with humorous, worldly eyes, she now shares her 1720 chateau "Vaulaville" with the public, keeping three rooms for guests at the top of her winding staircase and offering breakfast in the loveliest room I found in Normandy. In her salon, the walls are tinted green, and windows with high arches embossed with garlands of white flowers, look out on the lawn. What struck me was the contrast between the tales of brutality and humiliation she recounted to me, and the quiet peace of her formal rooms — the baroque clocks and inlaid desks, the sense of life acted out here generation after generation, in the same ordered, civilized way.

Order and civility were scarce commodities in 1940s Normandy when the war made a mockery of the familiar routines of family life. "By 1944, we were sick and tired of war, that's all!" says Marie Terese Osmond, who was then 16. "War was declared in '39, and my father left soon after. By '41, there was no gas for the cars and food and clothes were scarce. On weekends, our house became a pass-through for people coming down from Paris to hunt for what they couldn't find there. My mother tinted sheets to make clothes, my friend's father made shoes; we killed the calves."

"We could hear the bombing of St. Lô when it started."

For the people of Normandy, St. Lô was a name that sang of devastation. The Allies bombed it regularly from June 6 onward as the Germans made their stand there again and again; when the Allies finally took the town on July 19, it was a wasteland.

Canisy, only a few miles to the south and west of St. Lô, was a hot spot between two roads, with two bridges close by. "There was a month when first one side, then the other, had control," Madame Osmond recalls. One evening, her mother, who always milked the cows at dusk, came back from the barn, dropped the empty milk containers loudly on the kitchen floor and threw up her hands: "I can't sit and milk!" she exclaimed. "Bombs are whizzing through the barn!" Madame Osmond mimics her mother's anguished gestures, then drops her hands and adds wistfully, "The Germans came and, in one night, killed all my father's horses."

Today, Marie Terese and her husband, Roger Osmond, run a cozy *chambre d'hôte* on an enlarged small farm at St. Ebremond in the heart of the Calvados region, a rolling green sea that smells of apples and horses. She serves a lunch of homemade sweet apple chips and cider, and chicken stuffed with beans, prunes, shallots and liver; the *pièce de résistance* was *grandmere's* rice pudding.

"What's the secret?" I asked, peering into its rich brown lumpiness. "It smells divine!"

"After you've soaked the rice, then baked it slowly in non-pasteurized milk and sprinkled on a thick layer of sugar, you take an iron rod that's been heated red hot over the fire and move it around over the sugar topping until it turns into caramel." Another smidgen of Normandy forged by fire.

I find my next heroine, Elaine Gillet, in a Retirement Home in Paris. On the night of June 8, 1944, the Red Cross nurse-driver — unmarried, independent, with a family reputation for being "tempestuous" — responded immediately when called to leave Paris for Caen's Du Bon Sauveur hospital. She packed one bag and left that night; she was to be gone four months. She found Caen in flames, in a fire that raged for 11 days, burning out the entire city center. Gillet mopped up during and after the battle of Caen, which lasted over two months.

In a white silk blouse with her grey hair tucked under a transparent net, Gillet speaks without drama, in precise unhurried French, about her wartime job.

Most of it wasn't dangerous, she insisted. But once, a few weeks after D-Day, she was chauffeuring an unmarked car for a French Health Inspector in the countryside, when they found themselves under shrapnel fire from an English reconnaissance plane. "Suddenly the hood of the car shot up," she explained. "I felt like a red needle had gone through my cheek, but it was only the breath of a shell that was so close it burst my eardrum. Looking for cover, we got out of the car, crawled under barbed wire into an apple orchard, dove into a ditch and lay flat as soles."

"Soles?"

"Fish."

"I felt safe and happy under the apple trees," she adds, her voice high, remembering.

Gillet tells darker tales of severed limbs and painful deaths, many inflicted by British Typhoon planes, which had a range of over 600 miles. "The Germans suffered horribly," she says. "There were no planes for them, no tank offensive. When they went forward, they saw their equipment was not as strong as that of the enemy, so they dug trenches and got inside, to wait."

She leans back, eyes half closed, as if pulling out pictures in her mind.

"The fields were lush and green that summer and swarming with soldiers hidden behind the trees and hedgerows. It was the most amazing war," she offers, as if she has been thinking about it a long time. "Two of the strongest armies in the world, but most of the time, you saw no soldiers."

She was in *bocage* country, the vast inland areas that take their name from the 10-15 foot, thickly-entwined hedges found in many parts of Normandy. Used for centuries to mark off farmer's fields and keep livestock from straying, they were to the Allies what the jungles were in Vietnam — a hiding place for the enemy.

On my last day in Normandy, I hear of a woman who had been part of the Resistance. In the car my magazine has provided, I drive south of Avranches and make my way to Martrial Fouillard's door. In June of 1944, she lived with her husband and 15-year-old daughter on a farm near Marcilly, a place right on the Allied March.

Lean, agile, high cheek-boned, hair pulled tightly back, and looking starchy — but not 85 — Madame Fouillard leads me into her neat, spare kitchen. We sit across from each other at the table, and she brings out a folder of clippings and letters from Walter Costello, her last link to a heady time.

Walter was 24 in June 1944, a First Lt. from Georgia, flying a Mustang P51 which blew up over the roof of the Fouillard's neighbor's house. It was the American airman's first jump. The Germans saw the fire and came after the pilot — a dangerous search for the Fouillards who were already hiding three refugees — one French and two Russian. Madame Fouillard told me how she mustered her *sang-froid* and opened every bedroom door for the Germans — all "except the one where the Russians were hidden, close to the barn where we kept the weapons — two machine guns." Luckily, the Germans didn't move to the last door.

"Where did you get the weapons?" I ask.

"In the woods, ten kilometers away. American and British pilots dropped weapons for the Resistance."

"Why didn't they check every room, do you think?"

"Because God was watching," Madame answered.

The Fouillards at first hid young boys so they wouldn't have to work in the factories. Later their region's Resistance Coordinator placed other refugees with them; host and guest each knew his own role, nothing more, in case someone got caught.

On the day after the fire, they found Walter hiding in an unused quarry and offered to take him in. He stayed several days; then, they dressed him as a farmer and moved him by horse-cart "to the next place." All over France in those months there were hundreds of Walter Costellos, being adopted and then moved on by the wily Underground.

"He was crying when he left," Madame remembers. "He was having a good time with us, and he slept in a bed. Next place, no bed!"

A few days later, three Germans came to take the Fouillards' horses. When Madame Fouillard's husband refused, one of the Germans took a shot at him, grazing his cheek. Ivan, the refugee who was just finishing up supper in the next room, had heard enough. Germans had killed all of his family back home in the Soviet Union. He pulled a gun out of his boot and shot the three Germans dead.

"The problem, now," says Madame calmly, looking me square in the eye across the table, "was the three bodies."

"What did you DO?" I asked.

"We took them to the compost heap where we grew very tall cabbages. Not for us to eat, of course, but for the animals. We hid them there until it got dark."

"Then what?"

"We buried them in the garden."

"Three Germans?"

"Yes."

"Weren't they ever found?"

"No. Just after, came *La Débacle*. The Germans pulled out in a great hurry!"

This was the terrific advance of Patton's Third Army smashing the German Panzer counter offensive from Mortrain. Nothing could have hidden three missing men as effectively.

Before I leave, the Queen of *Sang-Froid* brings out a bottle of a red-wine liqueur, *Vin Cuit*. We lean across the checkered oilcloth, one lined face only a few inches from the other, waving our hands around in dismay at my bad French and her bad English. Then we raise our glasses to each other and drink to "precious *Liberté*" — words that both of us can understand.

"If you talk to Walter," she says with a sly smile, "tell him the young French lady does not forget him."

IV. Three From Indochine

Bronze, Walking Buddha, Sukothai style, 14th century.

It was the Asian art that drew me to Angkor. When Pol Pot's reign of terror ended in Cambodia, I found a magazine to buy a story proposal, a sidekick to hold my hand, and ventured forth to the treasures in the jungle.

The images of the stricken, lovely old peninsula stuck with me and lured me, in later seasons, on to Vietnam and Laos. The faces of the tough/gentle people, especially the clever Vietnamese who manage to connect without much language, are the surprises that pull me back.

By now, the Big Lessons are coming into focus: The farther I go, the longer I stay, the more obvious it is that the faces I look into are my own. The stranger is ME!

The farthest corners of the globe continually reaffirm the similarities of the human condition, show us that wherever we are, we are all sitting on the SAME rug.

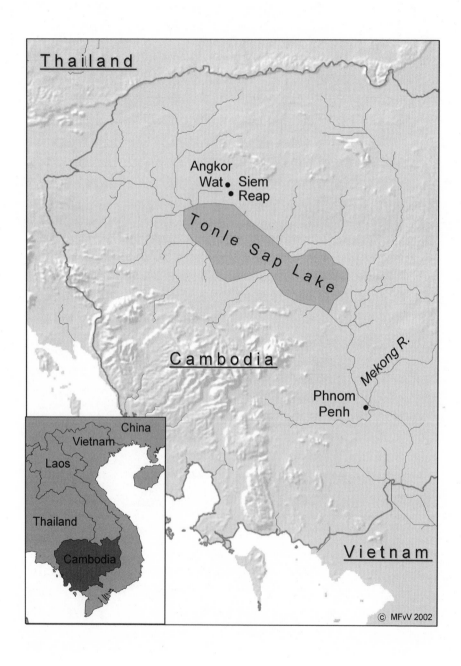

12   Tug of War Angkor:

Cambodia

In a tamed jungle setting in northwest Cambodia, scattered over an area of 60 square miles, more than 70 structures still exist in the complex of ruined capitals known as ANGKOR. The vast, rambling site was the heart of the Khmer Empire, where a dynasty of 25 kings — from the 9th to 14th centuries — created its monuments and ruled over a domain that included what is now Kampuchea, southern Laos, southern Vietnam and eastern Thailand.

After the last kingdom collapsed in 1431, tropical growth crept in and covered its mysteries until Henri Mouhot, the French naturalist, paddled up the Tonle Sap ("King's Lake") in 1859 — looking for butterflies, we are told — and saw in the distance ahead the five tall beehive towers of Angkor Wat (just one of the many sites). He wrote in his journal that the building must have been "erected by some ancient Michelangelo." It was, he said, "grander than anything left to us by Greece or Rome." Mouhot's remarks are still a true evaluation of Angkor Wat — as well as of the entire complex and all the other amazing edifices that have since been uncovered and partially restored. For all its present state of ravishment, the site has no equal in the world — as a cosmic scheme, as an engineering feat, as an aesthetic treasure, as an enclave of imaginative power.

Today, the long causeway entrance to Angkor Wat (the most reknowned and best preserved temple) stretches over a moat, now dry but once floating with guardian crocodiles, and still lined by a garland of mammoth serpent balustrades that from time to time rise up to display their many-headed cobra hoods. When a Khmer walked along this stone pathway, he was crossing one of the seven great seas of the Hindu cosmology, on a bridge that carried him from earth into heaven.

I had long imagined following the same worn path — and finally, in 1992, I was here. I had meant to come upon it in a cool dawn, but now a humidity factor of 100 per cent, with a temperature of 97 degrees, almost blocks any celestial vision I might conjure up. The sun bouncing off the shadeless sandstone has turned the stroll along the

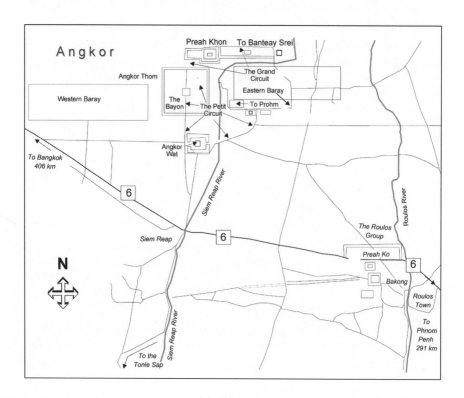

475 meter avenue into a divine ordeal. Eventually, I find myself on the other side and manage to crawl up the thigh-high steps, so awkward they must have been built with only the gods in mind, into the protective shade of the first terrace. There, I collapse, breathless, in front of Angkor's most famous story-in-stone, its pivotal creation myth: The Churning of the Ocean of Milk.

Rendered in precise bas-relief 50 meters long, the etched scenario runs horizontally along the wall of the Eastern Gallery. Though exposed on its weather/eastern side, it has been protected through the centuries by the gallery's overhanging roof as it hugs the inside, western wall. Finely chiseled into the blue/green sandstone, 80 devils on one side and 92 *devas*/gods on the other are engaged in a tug of war, each trying to churn the world out of the Milk of Chaos. Each side fights for the first drop, the ambrosia that is the elixir of life. For this Olympian job, they use as a rope the giant sacred serpent that they imagine entwined around the churning stick of the central tower of Mt. Meru (Angkor Wat).

As I move on through the dusky passageways, the stones seem to flow with me, gaining in potency as their three tiers rise in height. I have the sensation of being in a building that is a piece of dynamic sculpture.

The monuments at Angkor were originally the products of a Hindu civilization transplanted in 800 AD from Java to Indochina. With the exception of Banteay Kdei, built for the monks in the king's service in the 12th century, they were not created as habitations for man. They were a landing space for the gods. The Khmers believed in an intimate relationship between their mythical universe and the earth. By reproducing the Ideal on earth, man opened a gate for the gods, assuring harmony between the two worlds, without which humanity could never prosper. In the six centuries of Khmer rule, each king did some building, erecting a temple honoring his favored gods, himself or his family.

Gate, Angkor Thom, Jayavarman VII (1181-1201).

Now, on a typical four-day tour organized by Angkor Tourism, and traveling with my old family friend, Charlie, a serious photographer, I leave our hotel in Siem Reap, two miles from the ruins, to drive out each morning along the river where men are putting out fish traps and the red-dirt roads are full of rubble and rebuilding. Our 28-year-old guide, Rith, tells us he lost both his teacher-parents in "Pol Pot time" — 1975-79.

Along a paved road shaded by thick greenery, which the French called "*Le Petit Circuit*," we turn through one of the great directional gates surrounding the complex called Angkor Thom. Looking up at its towers, we are dazzled by the decoration — climbing 20 meters Rith says — into the leafy, filtered light, the dark sandstone blocks deeply carved all the way up. Stone elephants with their slack trunks at rest in front of them, seem to be holding up the towers of gigantic God-King-Buddha faces. Through this arch, built high enough for a Khmer king to parade under on his largest elephant, open-faced Cambodians of today call out "hello!" as they pass through — no hands! — on their bicycles.

We encounter another version of the tug of war in the form of massive sculptures along each of the North, South, East, West gateways of Angkor Thom. Many of the gods and demons are headless, armless, or eaten by a deadly white mold; some are whimsically framed in vines; others look sadly abused, as if their heads had been whacked off by vandals and put back on askew.

In the story, from the Hindu holy book, "The Mahabarata," it is the demons who win and snatch the first drops of elixir away — and that's why we have chaos in the world! I think about this here at Siem Reap, where guerrilla war has persisted for over 20 years, and chaos and evil have often raged, unbridled.

In four days, we see 27 of the major sites listed in our guide books. We view one or two of those thought to be less significant, from the car; but we get out and walk around most of them.

Wherever we are, Charlie has to climb every step to the top level. All echo some form of the temple-mountain, a summit where the king intercedes for his people. What they all have in common are steep steps and walls filled with lively carvings.

The exuberance of the Khmer art is a delight — sensual, but without the eroticism of India: *apsuras*/dancing girls; guard dogs; lions; the ever-present elephants and cobras, and that detached mythical beast, associated with waters and fertility, the *makara*, whom we encounter on stone stairs and over lintels, either disgorging or ingesting the world. Garuda birds with their strong, squat, feathered man-bodies lift their wings at every corner, ready to fly right out of the brick into my arms. When we visit Sra Srang, the still-green King's bath, another heavenly spot, we can recreate the irrigation system that the Khmers imposed on a once-arid savannah, redirecting and holding waters from the natural lake of Tonle Sap, inflated with each rainy season. Here, guardian lions still roar into a vast reservoir where farmers now plant rice, and remnants of the *naga*/snake, Angkor's most persistent signature, enclose its damaged terraces — the snake whose home is in the life-giving waters and whose shape can imitate the rainbow and the bridge to heaven.

In the predawn of our second day, we wait for the light to ascend on the 47 towers of the Bayon, the temple erected in the center of the complex of Angkor Thom by Angkor's greatest builder, Jayavarman VII (1181 — 1218.) It is quiet except for the sound of a dove and the clicking of a ghekko lizard. We have it to ourselves except for an old caretaker. This is how one needs to go: early and alone.

Slowly, we follow the sun to the eerie third level with its 172 gargantuan Bhudda-like faces. As we walk around, hundreds of eyes peer down on us at once. This king espoused Buddhism and, researchers think, envisioned himself as an aspect of the Bodhisattva of Compassion, a lord like its builder who was omnipresent and omnipotent — with eyes seeing in all directions. I found the unnerving scrutiny anything but compassionate, and the walkways within the Bayon itself, an enclosure inviting sorcery. The passageways, self-contained and narrow, run along a series of walls where one must bend low to view the stories in the stone; it's a place where anything could happen. I found it hard to leave. "Just one more cryptic smile," I begged, "caught from another slant of light, perhaps the next one more forgiving."

We are followed into the temples by touching waifs in cleanish rags, selling Cokes in coolers, and cowbells made from bamboo stalks. Toddlers present us with colored rocks and blooming weeds, and old men sell rubbings from the bas-reliefs in the temples. We take pictures of yoked bullocks plowing, sap oozing out of teak trees, and a tiny, wrinkled woman, squatting on the grass to smoke a fat cheroot.

To try to keep the city ruins from crumbling back into the mulch of the jungle, assistance has come from all directions. The French followed Mouhot's discovery of the area and have done the major rebuilding, especially of Angkor Wat; but Poland, India, Japan, America, and others are also present, each with its own project. Work is uneven, and Angkor's enemies have been devious and persistent: Underground water seepage, which threatens the stability of all their buildings, is considered the most serious now, but pestilential fungi — mold that eats into the stone — and lichen are almost as hard to deal with. Controlling the strangler fig and other predator trees is yet another challenge. Of all of the killer demons, only vandalism has been curtailed, as there's very little left to steal that isn't sunk in the earth. Most of the freestanding sculpture has been taken off long ago — by Cambodia's ancient enemy, Vietnam, and by the Khmer Rouge — some of it, we were told, turning up in European museums.

We never get to Banteay Srei, done in the 10th century, which art historians consider the jewel of Khmer art; it is off-bounds when we are there — too close to where the Khmer Rouge are presumed to be hidden in the woods. So we save our last good-byes for the place where we started, Angkor Wat.

As we start out, it is faintly drizzling. Charlie climbs high, while I wait out the shower in a first-level doorway. Leaning on a many-headed cobra hood, with a small Cambodian boy watching over me, in a few moments of perfect quiet, I am back again in the profound silence of the stones — in the emptiness of the massive structure — sensing the pull between the heavenly ideal of this place, and its dreadful, historical opposite.

The battle between good and evil is so real, it is as if my own arms are engaged in tugging on the hefty serpent. I imagine its scaly body slithering around the base of the sprouting lotus-bud tower, Mt. Meru, just up there. The aged stones of the building shudder as the giants yank the snake one way, then another, trying to force out the juice of life and maintain heavenly order. After four days permeated by this struggle, I understand the myth is not so much "a story," as a reflection of Angkor's history — then and now.

Showers begin again as we leave. The long causeway is slick underfoot and, in our last look back, we see children racing towards the dark blossoms of the five-mountain cosmos, their forms mirrored in the worn, wet stones.

Children racing towards the cosmos, Angkor Wat.

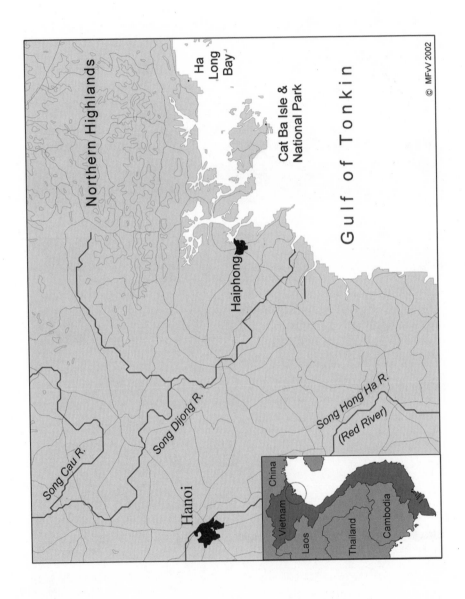

13   Brushing Past:

Vietnam

I was curious about Vietnam.

Like most Americans over 50, my idea of the country was largely formed by 20 years of news and TV headlines. Vietnam was a familiar map, littered with unpronounceable names that all sounded the same; my memories were of "experts" with "inside information" furiously arguing on every front, and — much too late — the awareness of the sickening quagmire. The finale was the returning vets — the story in their strungout faces — and the memorial in D.C. that was a light bulb, revealing the scope of the tragedy.

On the West Coast, where I live, the Boat People arrived and opened spare, cheap restaurants where we flocked to eat Lemon Beef Salad and bananas *flambe*. They sent their offspring to the state universities where, more often than not, they graduated in the top third in the sciences and math and were the first recruits that Bell Lab and Hewlett Packard picked up.

Any apprehensions about what it would be like in Vietnam were squelched by the pull I felt towards this foreign culture which was now part of our American history. It wasn't long before I had my visa stamped in my passport and was flying Cathay Pacific out of Hong Kong. As I heard the landing wheels of the plane drop over the Hanoi airstrip, however, I was surprised to find my confidence sinking with them.

I was beginning to wonder how I would be accepted. Maybe I should try to pass myself off as a Canadian, or a Swiss — someone who couldn't be blamed for the effects of Agent Orange or the craters in the rice fields?

On the ground, my thrifty Vermont friend Preb meets me with a bargain rental car, a tired Russian model. The air is warm and damp for the three-quarters of an hour it takes us to reach Hang Trong Street, just off Hoan Kiem Lake. Tamarind trees line the roads that are teaming with two-wheeled traffic, noisy with horns and tricky to cross. On foot, we turn between the small shops, off the sidewalk, through an arch, walking over broken tile and rubble, up a stone stairway, three flights. There, our room has a 20 foot ceiling with a balcony overlooking the street.

On the first morning, an odd rhythm interferes with my sleep. It is the sounds from the 6:00 AM sidewalk T'ai Chi class going on under my window. All of its members are women, with the leader calling the steps. On the second morning, I look across and recognize Phoung, who, yesterday, had brought us our morning coffee, French bread and cream cheese. In the third gray dawn, I stand on our balcony across from them and try to follow their exercises.

From our simple quarters, we have a natural window into the ordinary life of Hanoi. Our room adjoins a Community Center with a theater and restaurant on the terrace-balcony level that overlooks the Red River. When I think of the few days I spent in Hanoi, I am back in this place.

After walking the fast-moving, colorful, hot streets (which, I learned later, had not acquired streetlights until 1994) I return here at dusk. Some evenings, I have to edge my way across the theater floor, through the middle of a teenagers' karate class, to reach the stairs and a table at the Five Royal Fish eatery. There, trying out the local beer and savoring every claw of the lightly-fried soft-shelled crabs, I watch these young men go through their balletic practices.

The beat of a *passe* tune drifts up, along with the unmistakable aroma of a sweet weed. Some boys work the punching bags along the wall. Most are out in the middle, rehearsing in small groups, going over darts and thrusts and whole-body twists and stretches. Every one of their muscles seems to have learned the motions by heart, and I am mesmerized by their grace and panache. In their oversized white cottons, they are white bats, darting through the enclosing dusk.

In my balcony seat, I lean in as close as I can, thrilled to be on the front row of this indigenous show. I look hard. I listen hard — as if by paying close attention, I can catch the essence of this city, still largely unknown in the West. As if by a force of will, I can make the Red River spill out its secrets. When I leave, down the winding staircase, across the floor and back to my room, an early Leonard Bernstein marches me out. Fast fists pound the leather and lithe limbs hit the air, as I brush past them into the night.

The whiff of Communism is difficult to catch in Hanoi. While the massive, ugly mall leading to Ho Chi Minh's Mausoleum, with its Changing of the Guard performed in goose-step, does suggest Lenin's tomb in Moscow, the market is dominated by every kind of private business, zealously engaged in by every member of the family: food stands on the street where Mom sits all day making a large, thin, milky pancake that she fills with toppings; kids selling post cards and crude copies of Graham Greene's *The Quiet American* and the haunting poetry of *The Sorrow of War* by the Hanoi-born soldier, Bao Mihn, both best sellers on the street and translated into several languages.

The city is old and easy, its flavor accessible without guidebooks. Some French Colonial houses endure, evoking a gentler time — pastel colors, wide, protecting, outside shutters. Streets in the old part of town feature one product or service, the residue of a system that harks back to the original Thirty-Six Guilds of the 15th Century: the Shoe Street; the Tin Street; the Rope Street; the Silk Street; each sells its particular wares; and a street raining marble dust where in every cubicle workmen are carving tombstones.

Hanoians, on the whole, leave you to yourself. Shop keepers greet you with a big "Hello!" or "*Bonjour!*" but they don't nag. They let you browse; and they are infinitely solicitous. If they don't have the silk sleeping bag liner that you ask for, they will order you to "Wait! Just wait here!" — run two blocks down, find it in another shop and bring it back to you. (I got a wave-away gesture and exclamation, "No money!" when, once, I tried to re-pay for extra service and kindness.)

"What is your country?" the *cyclo* driver asks. When I mumble — sheepishly, the first time — "America," he is surprised — not many of us here yet.

"Oh! America!" he answers, his voice on a rising note. "GOOD country!"

All over Vietnam, they ask me how old I am. Once, when I answer, "Seventy-one," the man, who has a worn, plain face and is a veteran who doesn't want to talk about the war, responds with verve.

"*Chung!*" he says. The word means "strong." (It's the only Vietnamese word I came home with.)

Old means *strong* in a poor country like Vietnam where the thread of life is tenuous. In the Temple of Literature, the most precious stele in Hanoi rests on the back of a tortoise, a creature who symbolizes strength and longevity and is deep in the folk tales of the country. Old, I found out, was good. Confucius taught them that.

Seventy-one was the right age to be there. I was a tortoise.

But strength and tortoises have their limits, and I met mine on an island called Cat Ba.

Biker rests in front of Tortoise Pagoda, Hoan Kiem, Hanoi.

"I knew you'd want to see Halong Bay," Preb told me, "so I signed up for a weekend boat tour."

I'd read about this Must See destination, Vietnam's most spectacular landscape, northeast of Hanoi.

"It'll be a zoo," Preb said. "We might want to get off on our own afterwards. Maybe stay on and explore Cat Ba Island. It's a National Park, most of it still undeveloped, I think."

Everyone who has longed to see the mysterious humps of Guilin, China, goes on an excursion around Halong Bay. It's a natural wonder of three thousand limestone outcroppings — gray, sharp, treeless, something Faust might have pushed up on a bad night. The Vietnamese refer to these hills as the "ascending dragon." To echo the metaphor, all the wooden sightseeing boats show off a prow of a carved dragon's head, painted in bright, primary colors.

Ten-year-olds row scows alongside with coral, shells and gifts-from-the-sea jewelry to sell (shades of Dal Lake, Kashmir); King shrimp from its waters are the lunch treat; family houseboats, junks with orange sails, glide in close, and smiling children hang over the side and wave as we pass. The water world one meets is a delight; and it's bringing international currency into the local economy.

On the other hand, we had trouble getting the straight story about where and when the Cat Ba island ferry left; the local entrepreneurs, eager to be tour guides themselves, don't give out much information to the independent traveler.

If one manages, accidentally, to arrive at takeoff time, he finds a plank of driftwood stretched between the boats and the dock. The trip takes three hours, from Haiphong, and it's a working boat. The decks are piled with supplies for the homemaker, including new furniture, unpackaged, ready for delivery. After we get under way, children nap in the green-felt well of a pristine pool table destined to adorn some recent pleasure palace.

"Looking for a hotel?" inquires a young man on the way over. "When you get off, turn right and ask for my friend Kinh." He hands us a note, and as we pull closer to the harbor, points to a sprawling, concrete-block affair on the shore.

But Kinh is watching too. He has spotted us disembarking and is suddenly there, introducing himself. Charming, in pleated raw-silk trousers, and a silk shirt open at the neck, he is elegant enough for the front desk at the Oriental in Bangkok.

"The *Lonely Planet* guidebook says your hot water is iffy," mumbles Preb, never a pushover for charm.

"Old book!" says Kinh. "We have hot water now — and electricity."

He makes sure we don't go astray. (Imagine! Two tortoises, looking for comforts!) He urges us along the seawall walk and up his stairs — proud to show off his Double Rooms-With-A-View, for $12. His faucets spout steamily and he assures us that the electricity will come on after 6:00 PM. We sign on for two nights, spellbound by the astounding view from the balconies.

Cat Ba harbor is chock-a-block with tiny boats and picturesque beyond belief with its improbable outcroppings of dragons, undulating behind the bustle. The new family hotels and one paved road hug the shoreline. Entertainment is a motorbike ride out to see the sunset. The island economy seems to be poised between subsistence aquaculture and the promise of a tourist hot spot. For the traveler who wants to be there first, Cat Ba island is a find.

Kinh brings out his brochure of possible excursions, complete with color photos. We pick a "half-day" trip — a trail that crosses the island, rises to a view of "all of Halong Bay," then drops down the other side, where a boat with a lavish buffet lunch awaits. We glance at some pictures of jockish youth, wearing muscles and backpacks, whose testimonial reads: "Grand view at the top makes it worth the grueling climb."

That should have been the tipoff, but we weren't receiving the message. Our hubris was on overdrive.

Where I come from in California, "National Park" means the strenuously-pruned trails of Pt. Reyes and Yosemite. Preb, ex Peace Corps, is ready for anything; Suyen, who signed up with us, is a fierce Dane and just a kid at 50; the fourth of our quartet is Lynn, 60-just, who is traveling by bicycle, one she had brought over from England. We all knew we could handle it.

I am on the back of a motorbike, behind a youth whose name I haven't yet learned. Following, each on her own bike, sitting behind a driver, are Preb, Suyen and Lynn. We have just met our guide, Miet, who is slight, smiling, confident. We are all on our way to the Park entrance to begin our walk.

The morning is drizzly and the road, winding. We are not going fast, but my driver skids on the wet pavement, flying off onto the hard surface. His knee takes the fall.

In slow motion, I put out my left hand, skidding off behind onto my well-padded hip. The motorcade behind us stops. Preb whisks out bandages and disinfectant and washes off the gashed knee. I have nothing but a scrape on my palm. We hover over the wounded driver until one of the Vietnamese puts him on another cycle and takes him off to the town clinic.

Shaken, but relieved that nothing worse has happened, we remount and continue on. I hold the next driver a bit tighter around the waist. "You are a lucky bum!" I brag to myself.

Soon, we have dismounted again, said goodbye to our drivers and started, on foot, walking up hill. It's damp. No sun. Woodsy in places, more open in others. Up several hills we go, over sharp, black, slippery rock, then down the other side over lookalike black, slippery rocks. This is where I begin to slow down.

I can't seem to get my footing, keep scraping my ankles, my arms, my shins. We push past dark green, long, shiny leaves that hint of old news-clips of jungle warfare. The trail is often obscure. "We could use a machete," I think more than once. It's a tough go.

As the hours tally up (we learn later that we covered 16 kilometers) my legs don't seem to be working right. I slip and slide, bang elbows, ankle-bones and surfaces I didn't know I had on my rear end. At 2:00 PM, lunch time on the boat, we are still ascending and famished. Preb makes us stop and eat the bread and cheese she has brought, just in case. Standing still and leaning on wet rocks, we are a target for a myriad of inquisitive leeches, the itty brown kind that reach out towards warm, dark crevices.

Various parts of me begin to ache, and I get colder and stiffer. I feel like a knight in rusting armor; soon I won't be able to move. I begin to meditate on hot tubs and feather beds. As the hours wear on, I am fixated on lying down.

We never see the top or the view. In the Scotch Mist, it eludes us. By now, we just want to get there, wherever "there" is. The light is beginning to fade. We don't talk much as we begin to go down. In time, we come to a wide valley, a village, and people. We take pictures of a girl in a straw hat with flowers. We buy Cokes. It is, after all, just an ordinary day hike on an island in Halong Bay. As we cross the rice fields in the dusk and take off through more trees, the trail is still rocky and, within half an hour, we are moving in the dark.

It's about now that Miet takes charge. He comes over and grips my left arm, propelling me forward. Slipping and sliding our way over loose rock, we stumble to sea level. I am as drained as I have ever been. I can't see much, but can hear the water lapping. Predictably, the boat is not there; we are five hours late for lunch.

I sit down on a rock and take deep breaths, feeling seasick and dizzy. Something odd is going on, but I am too busy staying vertical to think it through.

As if it is happening offstage, I realize Miet is going into action. He calls in a high-register voice, making bird noises into the woods, at the same time waving his flashlight up and down.

"How hopeless!" I think. "Who will see or hear that!?"

But someone does respond. A boat shortly appears, a rowboat with a woman bailing. The import of the boat's shortcomings registers only later. We all get in. I take a deep breath: "Incredible luck holding out!" I intone.

But we don't go far. Only Miet knows where we are, and he knows we need a better boat. Suddenly, we have pulled up along the side of a sharp rock ledge where a family are camped under a blue tarp tent. "Why are we doing this?" I ask the night, or anyone who will listen. They open their flap, pull us in, make way for us on their straw mats and offer us peanuts and apples. The scene has a dream quality, but it's not a nightmare. This is a temporary haven. Rescue is at hand.

Another boat arrives, men in beige uniforms, the Park Service. They can get us a boat with a motor, for $30. We all nod in unison and soon a coracle appears before us. We get in and sit with heartbeats on hold as the motor refuses to catch. At last, it turns over, and our basket ship is skimming, fast, over cobalt water.

On the water, no lights, no markers lead the way; our craft carries one "Donut Ring" attached to a rope, but no lifejackets. We sit hunched down, ducking the wind, on damp planks — silent, cold and apprehensive — for almost two hours. For me, the aura is surreal; we might as well be on Starship One: our navigators — our rescuers — our old enemies, the ones we called "Gooks" and "Commies."

The dragon hills loom closer. The shapes are as powerful — as divine — as the East has always found them. Here and there, a star hangs in the valley between the segments of their angry, frothing tails.

Separated from my accustomed self, I hang with them, dreaming on an unexplored level — an ink blot lost on a *sumi* scroll — part of the "ten thousand things," the deep deep, and the suspended stars.

Without warning, we wake up to the thump of wood against our bow. The stars have gone and we are blinded by the harsh florescent bulbs on our home-dock.

Kinh is there, and his worried face moves in close. He is almost hysterical, peering into each of our faces, one by one, needing tangible evidence that we've returned without scars.

"Are you all right?" he asks, and for the first time, I know I'm NOT. I must have hurt myself in the fall from the bike, all those hours ago. When he sees that he has to do most of the work getting me up and over the gunwales, he gives a dark, soulful chuckle.

Time speeds up again, and it's only minutes before he has gathered us all back for tea and beer in his warm lobby. As I drop, dead-weight, into one of his oversized sofas, relief rolls into the room like the evening fog. You can hear my sigh in Hanoi.

The bruises came and went in ten days — lucky again, they were only bruises — but the new dimensions I saw in the sky that night, they aren't going away.

I crawl back to Hanoi, exhausted, chagrined. I have BECOME the tortoise. Every movement is a slow labor. My legs have grown shorter, my hide tough and leathery. I need to stay close to water, and my energy is on half. I hope someone doesn't fancy me for soup.

But I and my animal spirit, we still have some *chung* left in us. In a few days, we are ready to brave the overnight sleeper train to Hue and continue our journey down the east coast. I have reserved a Soft Seat, which I hope will live up to its name.

The train leaves at 10:00 AM. In my assigned compartment are four berths with three-inch foam, one heaped with bedding for the whole car, five men and myself — an inauspicious beginning.

With only a few common words, we try to talk. Van hands me his card. He is a representative of Vietnam Petroleum, "the

Boss," one of the others tells me. "This must be the new Vietnam," I think, "farmers in business suits." Plain, alert faces, careful behavior; I like them instantly and try to follow their lead.

We eat shredded beef and beans from partitioned, plastic boxes. Dessert is a banana. Afterwards, musing into the landscape, we practice toothpick technique. Toai, the one in the lavender shirt, pulls a stool into the passageway to smoke, directing his puffs out through the grated screen.

Outside, long shadows fall across the precise, green geometry of the fields. A silhouette of three bikes parked on the ridge of the furrows reflects into the wet around the new rice. We see rural Vietnam out the window — the effort it takes to live on the land without tractors and sprinkler systems. Behind the Annam highlands, the light turns pink, then charcoal; an old man, bony-thin, is still pushing his bullock-drawn plow through the mud.

Inside, I have staked out a guilty claim to a corner of a Lower bunk. I'm anxious because my ticket is for the Upper, but I doubt if I can get up into it.

By the time it is dark, the Boss is stretched out across from me, looking at my *Passport* guide. Two of the loiterers, originally trying out our space, have vanished; and all the sheets, pillows and quilts from the top bunk have been dispersed. Toai, who has told me he is 32, strips off his trousers and, underneath, has on discrete black tights. I can't help gawking at his tiny waist and am peeking as he straddles the canyon between the berths. Without any visible effort, he takes a long yoga stretch up from the metal step and swings himself onto the top berth.

"You will not have to sleep up there," Van assures me.

What a relief! Now I can relax. My head drops down on the Lower, but I am instantly admonished, "No! No! the other way!" all three cry together. "Not your head near the aisle. Not safe!"

"Toward the outside window?" I ask. "Yes, yes," they answer in unison. "Feet by the aisle."

Then, when we are all under our quilts and they have seen that my wallet and passport are under my head, the last one in turns out the overhead light and double-bolts us in. I never, ever, felt so safe.

At 3:30 AM when we arrive at the station in Hue, I have to wake Van because he has put my suitcase under the storage compartment beneath his bunk. "No problem," he mumbles amiably, pulling it out for me.

As I'm getting reassembled in the dark, the only treasure I've allowed myself, a silver choker, has slipped unnoticed off my neck and onto the floor. I'm on my way out, scrambling down the too-steep steps to the station platform, but Van has spotted the chain and calls out to me: "Ginny!"

He catches up to me, leans down from the train and lodges it firmly, deeply, between my hands. Then, with both HIS hands, he squeezes mine together in an extra-energetic hug and, pleased with his rescue — and I think with the exchange — seals the bond with a triumphant grin.

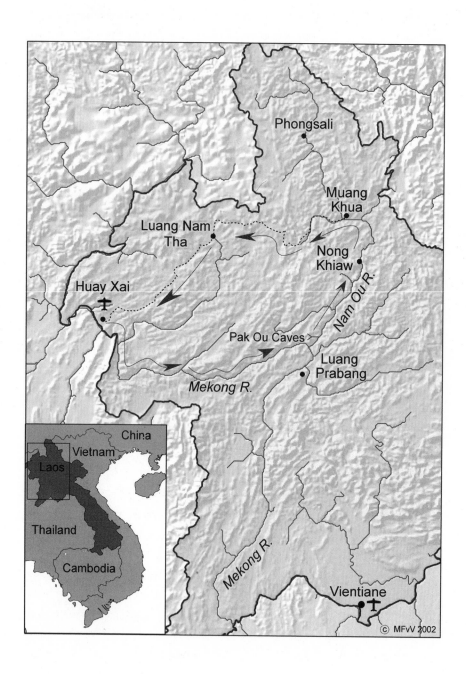

14   Seeker of Pearls:

Laos

In the south land many birds sing
Of towns and cities half are unwalled.
The country markets are thronged by wild tribes;
The mountain villages bear river names.
Poisonous mists rise from the damp sand;
Strange fires gleam through the night rain.
And none passes but the lonely seeker of pearls
Year by year on his way to the South Sea.
         — Wang Chien, 8th Century

It's been a long time since I fell in love with a man. Now I fall in love with rivers. The elements of entrancement are always the same. I have to be IN it, smell, taste and touch the water, feel the pull of its cool arms, peer into its whirlpools.

    I saw the mighty Mekong first in 1992 after driving all day through the mossy green of northeastern Thailand. Standing on its bank, looking out, it was a letdown: plain, wide, still, and colored bronze. Not much chemistry. It could have been the Mississippi, except that the boats were wrong and the darting eyes set in delicate Asian faces weren't Huck Finn's. It was slow to get under my skin.

But after my first trip to Vietnam, early in 1996, I kept wondering what was on the other side of the Annam Mountains, how I could cross them and get into hidden Laos, to the river that marks much of its eastern border. That's when the idea of the muddy swath — the river of life, the river of blood (it's been called everything) became a Lorelei.

The maps of the rivers of Indochina were as luscious as if some watercolorist, stuck in the stacks of the Geological Surveys, had poured them onto the pages. In bed at night, before departure, buried under a swirl of cartography, I imagined my cargo boat as a mighty paintbrush, cutting a swath through the Mekong, froth and foam cutting across our wake, taking us past the shining rocks and deep-water pools caught in our binoculars.

Over many weeks, I conceived a grand scheme, gathered three hardy friends to join me along the way and took off in March for Vientiane, the capital and only legal port of entry for international flights. On the map, an unlikely airport was marked, at Huai Xai, 150 kilometers south of the Chinese border, which I later learned had been built by the C.I.A. I wanted to fly up there and go south, by any old boat we could find, perhaps as far as Cambodia, a journey of over 1000 kilometers. Two guidebooks assured me that the 549 kilometers of river to the north and south of Vientiane, were navigable year 'round.

As planned, we flew into Vientiane and went out on our first evening to catch the sunset on the river from the Mixay Cafe, a popular eating place hanging over its banks. There, I got a dry, stinging slap in the face!

The mighty Mekong had become a far distant trickle of water flowing around the outer edge of a long, wide sandbar where boys fished with handheld nets in ankle-deep water for tiny fish, perhaps bait, we supposed. Unless we departed like Winkin', Blinkin' and Nod, in a shallow paddled pea-green scow, we weren't going to go far over this low water.

It wasn't happening, not this late in the year. We had to revamp the game plan. If we couldn't travel over the central part of Laos by boat, we would cut it out like an ailing intestine, spend more time in the north and the south. We started by flying north to the UNESCO World Heritage site of Luang Prabang.

By now, we are a critical mass. In Hanoi we added a young New Yorker to the original core-group of three from California and, at the airport, were joined by a brother and two sisters from Washington D.C. (one a Peace Corps volunteer serving in Thailand who spoke some Thai). From various sources, we are all following a Guest House lead and share an open jitney from the airport. When we arrive, we almost fill the place with its half a dozen rooms. Each one of us a scoffer at "groups," we have by now formed one of our own.

The charming, worldly-wise Phunong manages the PA PAI GUEST HOUSE. Our nameless street is residential, with trees and pots-in-planters, lined by French-style wide-shuttered houses in pale tints — no traffic except an occasional bicycle and the ice cream vendor pushing his cart. We are on a rise, where we look, directly across the street, down on the entryway to one of the minor Buddhist Wat/temples, whose rituals begin to mark our day.

I wake with the 4:30 AM gong, try to sleep til the next one at 7:00. Over strong coffee, fresh pineapple, yogurt and French bread in the courtyard, I eye the young monks, vivid in orange, as they lounge on their whitewashed entryway steps. I come to know their thong-shuffle, the repeated gesture of rewrapping the shoulder piece of their robe and the quick snap of raising their sun-umbrellas as they take off on their rounds. I never tire of this mime scene at the Wat Pa Phai. It brings the first moments of serenity that fall over me in Laos.

But I am not here for lolling on terraces. I am here for the river, and two days after we arrive in Laos, we are out ON it! Eight of us in a long-tailed boat with engines gimbal-mounted on the stern, dividing the price of $30 for a day's jaunt to and from the Pak Ou Caves, 25 kilometers upriver.

Our driver sits in front; his son Kip bails and looks out near the propeller in the rear for rocks and seaweed. We have open sides and a cover, with a space between the driver's station and the passengers' seats where two or three can stand, and from which, if the driver consents, it's an easy hoist up onto the long, flat roof.

On this day trip, we have added the Yorkshireman Philip, met in a restaurant one evening; the rest are Americans, ranging in age from 72 to 27. The man who brokers the boats and some drivers have a few words of French and English, but mostly, we get by with sign language.

Once we are on the water, the raw edges of our disparate personalities begin to wear down; as the river flows past — every second a changing shoreline, a changing sky — we are forced to operate in the moment: to be, to see, to abandon both what came before and what may come after. We can sit, or stretch out inside, have room to rest, write, read, photograph, think! We carry our own food, water, hats and sunscreen, which we share with each other and the driver.

The Mekong begins wide and brown, following a clearly marked channel of concrete blocks that show its varying depths; the top markers are always painted red. I thought of them as lighthouses. We see boats of all kinds, including a few noisy speedboats with helmeted passengers. Veggie gardens dot the steep alluvial river's edge, each plot marked from its neighbor by a bamboo partition. Children at every village's waterfront show off, splashing and screaming as they see our boat pass by. A long, shallow boat loaded down with green, stripped melons passes close; a woman, enveloped in the fruit, ducks her head down under a stripped umbrella. I have missed the photograph, but the picture is caught in my memory.

By mid afternoon, we have arrived at the caves, where — at its confluence with the Nam Ou River — clear, aqua water pours into the muddy Mekong. The caves, high up off the river, are dark and holy, bursting with wall-to-wall buddhas. No commercial intrusions

Monk and Mekong, Luang Prabang.

have been allowed, and the site has remained oddly untouched by its daily stream of visitors.

At Luang Prabang, we don't stray far from the enchanting architecture and sculpture of the wats; some roof lines dip almost to the ground. There are few tourists, so far, mostly Europeans — *farangs* who nod to each other, passing on the streets, at the fax machine, bargaining for textiles with the Humong women, who vigorously peddle their antique needlework under the shade of a great tree near the post office.

The *tuk-tuk* drivers cruise close by, sometimes just pull up and wait by our steps; they know eventually we will get tired of walking around town in the heat. We go in a group to cool off under the sensational Kuang Si Falls; and, on another afternoon, I go to visit the grave of Henri Mouhot.

Mouhot is known as the "discoverer" of Angkor because he was the first Westerner to describe it, in an account published posthumously. He died right here in Luang Prabang in 1861, of malaria, at 35. He was coming back from Cambodia, on his way home to spread the secrets of the great temples. His village in France — Montbellard — raised the money for his memorial here and saw that his tomb was marked with a sweet tribute: *Fiere de son enfant*/proud of its son.

Our taxi driver is oblivious of the exact history, but understands the pride part. He knows he has a job leading visitors along the treelined, rooted path above the river, to the spot near the textile village, where the crypt rests, half covered with vegetation. In coming here, I am completing a tiny circle, within a much larger one, as my own glimpse of Henri's vision at Angkor just five years ago still stirs my imagination.

As March turns steamy in the city of Wats, the "Calling For Rain" Buddha, which is particular to Luang Prabang, seems to be stretching his arms directly out to me. I listen more carefully to the reports from other travelers about the Nam Ou River (redundant as "*Ou*" means "river"). Above the caves where we have just been, its water level may still be high enough for travel northeast into the tribal areas of Phonsali Province. It's a greener river, we hear, more dramatic and more intimately appealing than the Mekong.

As sweat fogs my glasses and I start risking ice in my tea, the name "NAM OU" hangs in the dank air, becoming an insistent mantra. Our Luang Prabang idyll is drawing to a close.

It is 7:10 AM and the rooster is crowing as Phunong serves us fruit in the courtyard of the Pa Phai. The D.C. family has left for the airport and, with my three seed-core compadres — Patricia & Adam from the West, Kim from Manhattan — I go to Immigration to get passports stamped (we are leaving Luang Prabang Province), and buy tickets to move farther north.

We find ourselves, with a dozen or so local men, women, children, produce — plus various birds, and one piglet, headed for the skillet — on the public boat #044 travelling up the Mekong and the Nam Ou to Nong Khiaw, which means "Green Pond." We can't pronounce it, but it's at the northern end of the loop that will land us on the upper Mekong at Huai Xai, my original destination.

On board with us are a newlywed couple from Milano — Mario, a John Lennon lookalike, and Ana, who paints small watercolors as we travel. The sound of water drowns out everything else: other cargo boats; our periodic stops at the floating gas stations; the vendors who come on board with greasy donuts for sale.

The hills we slide by are hazy, the vegetation lush — feathery. Later I hear that slash and burn farming permeates the dry season. Two young fishermen stand in a wooden scow, throwing out glistening plastic nets. On the banks, tiers of sand, like steps, run down to the river.

In a couple of hours, we are back up at the Pak Ou cave entrance.

Only a short distance beyond, the Nam Ou enters and once again, the bluer, clearer water mixes with the muddy Mekong — as if on a painter's pallet — and this time our expectations of it, wake us up.

Just around the bend from this exhilaration of moving over a new river, we feel a jolt, hear a funny noise in the stern: broken propeller. Long bamboo poles are brought out to steer us to shore; we are close to a sheer cliff, in a shallow inlet. While our driver and his helper get out and make repairs, a huge piece of clay falls from the bank and splashes mud on Kim's t-shirt. Apparently nothing is as stable as it might seem, but in minutes we are moving again — no time for any qualms.

The Nam Ou lives up to its seductive reputation. It's narrow; we skirt in and out of low, white water, clear water. Sometimes we can see pebbles on the bottom. Sometimes there's deep water and we make an impressive wake. Our driver squats barefoot on the crude planks in front of his wheel when he maneuvers the rapids. In the back, the Laotians pass out thin strips of sesame seaweed and try our cukes and tomatoes. Kim struggles with the sticky tamarind fruit while Adam dozes, his wrists entwined with string from a "blessing" ritual two days ago.

We pass a village every half hour or so, always high up, the palm-leafed huts built on stilts and barely visible through the jungle underbrush. Bamboo grows profusely, as does the opium poppy. We see both brown and pink/white water buffalo, camouflaged to blend with the low river rocks and sand. When the sun moves in, we all jump over the side in whatever clothes are handy, and the village comes out to cheer, and stare, standing on the rocks.

We arrive at a landing towards the end of the afternoon. Children swimming, women washing clothes, some boats, a steep, dry dirt hill. "Nong Khiaw?" we ask and are directed up the hill, not having any idea what to expect. Adam's pack is 45 pounds; but even my small rucksack and camera bag feel heavy. (If "tourist infrastructure" had arrived, there would have been someone here grabbing our bags and dispensing cards to Guest Houses, as in Vietnam.)

At the top of the hill, there is no sight of a green pond. We walk onto a wide stretch of packed, red dirt: the main drag. Whatever services exist in Nong Khiaw are on either side of it, along with the townspeople (if you could call it a town), a couple of roosters, baby chicks, a bike or two, a truck. A friendly woman ushers us into her guest house, but the rooms upstairs are little more than dog cages, close together, no air, no privacy.

Kim, our youngster in her twenties and never one to be defeated, blasts ahead up the road and finds a more encouraging place where we take two doubles with mattresses on the floor. From a "veranda" outside, steep wooden steps lead down to the back, where there is a squat toilet, drums of cool water and dippers, for a Mary Martin/"South Pacific" shower; and a tap where the family brushes teeth and does laundry.

Nong Khiaw was a stopping-off place on the loop north, west, south and then east, from Luang Prabang. My four friends and I covered this circle in nine days; ultimately, we paired up to experience parts of it, by boat, and by local taxi/buses (when the river was too low for boat traffic). Because of the constraints of fixed air tickets, and other personal considerations, none of us ever got as far northeast as Ponsali province, heralded as the place to see "timeless Laos" and tribals far from the reaches of ordinary tourism.

Now — when I think about our *Indochine* wanderings along the rivers in that late spring — or when someone asks me, "What was it like in Laos?" it is an image from the hours we spent at "Nong Khiaw" that comes back to me.

The hub of Nong Khiaw is the concrete bridge at the end of town, the only "modern" intrusion, except for its wayward electricity.

Between about six and sunset, whatever action there is in town, takes place on the bridge.

Everyone is here. Adults stroll across and look down at the drop of the river — at the rocks, the riffles — at what might be known as "the green pond" (we never find out) — at the blue-grey hills that move in and out of the tule fog. People stop in the center, hang over the rail, comment on the panorama and the news of the day. Children play games on the only smooth, paved roadbed they have; women dress for an evening "out," wear the handwoven, deep-bordered *phaa nung* skirt with a silver belt and a silk blouse, carrying their babies in colorful cotton slings. A boy races by with a piece of paper simulating an airplane. A man with a rifle over his shoulder "patrols," up one side and down the other. When the stars appear, teenagers sit close on the curb, one of them playing a flute.

The only Lao word we know is the greeting *Saibaaidi!* Unless we call it out, we are left to ourselves. But if we say it to any one we pass, an energetic chorus comes back to us: "*Saibaaidi! Saibaaidi!!*" — over and over, across the chasm between our cultures.

On the bridge, time hardly moves. Just before the night closes in, I see all of us, oddly, in soft focus, through a scrim. Not quite anywhere, but poised in a slow dance, with these people I don't know, can't ever know — with their dozens of tribes and a major language that has six tones and an alphabet that looks like bubbles.

Not quite anywhere, but entwined with these villagers on a Brigadoon bridge rising out of the damp sands — a bridge, which for a few improbable moments, seems to hover over the gray mizzle that has settled above the entrancing Nam Ou that evening.

Perhaps the dizziness, the sense of the surreal, aren't just a touch of Equatorial sun, or traveler's fatigue at the close of day. It could be that another tough tortoise is at work here — his precious antique shell crouched low as he hides himself behind the dank, dark boulders and concentrates on wickedly bewitching *another* lonely seeker of pearls passing by on the way to the South Seas.

Coda

Between the Cactus and the Sea:

Baja, Mexico

We have our fingers crossed as we drive along a rutted sandy lane that's barely passable in our low-slung rental car. Looking for a deserted Robinson Crusoe beach, we have, so far, been disappointed by Bahia Conception. The area offers miles of clean, shallow, safe water, lapping gently on a series of sand-strips, but many other campers have arrived here ahead of us. Now, on our second exploratory foray out of Loreto, we wonder at what instant our car will become bogged down in the sand.

Up ahead, we see a Y in the path, and, as we come closer, a sign low on the right hand side. It seems to be written by hand on a slab of fiberboard attached to a couple of uprights. It reads *Playa Perla*, which means Pearl Beach, and underneath, almost illegible, *palapas* for rent.

"*Palapa?*"

"You know, like a gazebo, only with the sand for a floor and made of palm leaves."

"Not my speed," I grumble.

We are a trinity of three generations: myself, "Granma," 75;

my daughter, Dorcy, 45; and Dorcy's five-year-old Alexander, a.k.a. Sandy. We have widely divergent interests, energies and preferences — but one gene we all appear to share is the one that bestows an impulse — if not an obsession — to push on to the end of the road, no matter how far or how risky.

With Dorcy at the wheel, Sandy and I egg her on to follow the ruts, which go up, down and around, through the unstable sand "road," as it weaves towards the beckoning sea — until we find ourselves moving out onto a plateau, overlooking the Sea of Cortez.

We look at each other — deeply, doubtfully. In a spare and lonely sort of way, the setting attracts us: a cove, turquoise water, white sand, with nothing much else in our line of vision.

"Could it be there is no one else here?" we ask in unison.

Our silver VW Bug looks so out of place it could be a paper decal cut out from a kids' sticker book and pasted on the picture of a desert landscape of ground up rocks and scrub. The sea is 50 feet below us, the horizon dead ahead. A few scattered structures are within eyesight; a wooden one, a little walk up the hill, looks like an outhouse. The others are the palm-frond windbreaks, *palapas* — three on the level we have driven in on.

Focusing, we notice a shack almost out of sight up beyond the outhouse. Looking down at the lower level, where a path goes down to a cove, we can see two RV's parked there and two more *palapas*, but not close enough to intrude.

Pretty soon Pablo — who we find out manages the campsite in this national marine preserve we have stumbled into — appears from his shack, the one almost out of eyesight. He's a wrinkled old Mexican with a toothless smile, kind eyes, about as much English as we have Spanish. The *palapas*, he tells us, rent for $5 a night each, or $25 a week. None of them is taken right now.

We hadn't known what we were looking for, exactly, but we have few doubts that this is IT. This place, bleak as it may appear, is "ours."

I readjust my thinking. I'll be a sport and try a *palapa* for a couple of nights. Maybe sleeping on the sand won't be intolerable. Anyway, I can always move up the road to a bed if my deteriorating bones protest too much.

Partly to keep anyone else from coming in close to us, we tell Pablo we'll take "*dos palapas por una semana.*" Pablo looks at us knowingly, as if he has encountered ridiculously extravagant Americans before.

Under one overhang, Dorcy helps me put my tent up next to the one she will share with Sandy; this, we decide, will be The Sleeping *Palapa*. The second structure, farther out on the point and windier, will be for cooking, eating, relaxing. We set about making it comfortable, using two abandoned tires for seats and setting up a makeshift table

The kind of *palapas* we have found at *Playa Perla* are 16 by 12 feet, three sided, with the fourth one open on the seaside. Pablo built them, starting with two rows of three upright limbs cut from the cactus, driving them deep into the sand. He notched each at the top and secured straight boards in the notches, to frame and stabilize the structure. Between the uprights, to make the walls and the roof, he used large palm leaves, overlapping them, weaving them in place with more palm strips and sometimes with wire and string. Right away, the interior ceilings and walls remind me of Leh, Ladakh, Jammu/Kashmir province, northern India, where I lived amongst blond wood with all the gnarls and imperfections showing.

As we settle in, a breeze comes up and we are happy to have a windbreak as we try to keep the temperamental sterno stove flame burning to heat up soup. The night heron, guardian of the dark, has just landed on his sentry-rock nearby. It's plain that the two flashlights hung from the ceiling will preclude reading after dusk, but the sunset that announces nightfall is so spectacular I forget to complain.

By the time we all crawl into our bags together, we all doze off, listening to the wind and the sea; I am conscious of our closeness to the raw elements, yet protected by the cove and the windbreaks. We are closer to each other than we've been in years — eggs touching in a nest, close enough to feel each other's pulse.

Daybreak is an event. The change in the light wakes me and I unzip the top section of my tent "window." The sun peeps up over the horizon, spreading out a pink, red or orange sea before it. Soon after, Sandy's face takes its place, peering in, nudging me awake to read him a story.

As our days at *Perla* drift into one another, the happenings of each day become recurring images that mark every day — notes of a reverberating tune.

The first activity of the morning is the trip to the bathing and tooth-brushing pool. It's out the tent flap, left, and down over a rocky path we have cleared. Ahead is a pool where the water level rises and falls with the tide. I sit on one rock and Sandy sits on the other. We have soap and a towel and try to be good campers and not pollute. More often than not, a Heerman's gull, the one with the yellow beak, tries to hog the pool. As he sees us coming down, he squawks loudly, retreating to a rock farther out that we can't reach. Sometimes his mate joins him and the two of them complain. They're right: it's not our space.

The second portion of each day is devoted to cornflakes and fruit in the dining area, and surveying the crescent beach below. We wonder if Pablo, whose boat is anchored here, caught any fish when he went out at dawn or found any treasures in his traps?

Early afternoon is the time to consider the sun, the wind, the tide and go on the second excursion of the day, down to the cove to sunbathe and swim, maybe look for improbable fish among the rocks. The Magnificent Frigate bird with the forked tail glides overhead as I lie back and pull my straw hat down over my nose. Its circling drift imitates my slowed-down breathing. What I see as I peek out would not have thrilled me in the past.

In 1977 and the years after, when I first started wandering and felt the sense of discovery pulling into a harbor in the Hebrides, or rounding a turn on the Annapurna loop and catching the sight of a white-topped mountain up ahead, this flat bleakness would not have been my oyster. I wanted exotica then, the stranger, the better. I longed to come upon a statue of Vishnu in a field, stretched out, asleep on an enormous snake, dreaming the world — shudder at orange goats' heads on sticks in the Kathmandu markets — or suddenly catch the whiff of yak butter.

But, in this recent winter month in Baja with my next-of-kin, I am perfectly in tune with the nearly vacant terrain, just as I was with the calm vistas of nothing I saw from the Laos rivers, a couple of winters ago. This too turns out to be a discovery of untried boundaries. After all the adrenaline-pushing charges of the test-ing years — after all the leaps in the dark — here I am in the brightest sunlight, peeking out through the filter of my straw hat, at an undramatic, almost blank canvas.

The most notable sight for those of us who don't often visit the desert — in their own way as awesome as the Callanish *men* — is the forest of incredibly big *cardon* cactus, some over 60 feet tall. An army of these giants clusters along a trail just south of us. The her-ons and pelicans guard our front, sea-flank, and the cactus our rear flank. We live, for this time, between the cactus and the sea.

As the sky turns deep purple, we head out to investigate the three or four restaurants near us along Route One. When we ar-rive, we know we are in Mexico. The shacks are gathering places for the local residents, and gregarious Dorcy babbles to everyone in her own crude bilingual mix. We attract attention, a *gringo* family traveling together with a blond *nino*. In no time, we find passing trucks waving to us, greeting Sandy by his official name, *"Alejandro! Que tal?"*

As we drive back to our camp after supper, we catch the tag end of a feathered sunset etched over the dark ridges of moun-tains that run down the center of the Baja peninsula. Just before downtime, Moon Viewing is the last order of the day. On one night, when the moon is full and as close and bright as a paper lantern, we celebrate its radiance by singing every "moon" song we can remember and taking photos. Developed, these come out with the moon looking tiny. You had to have been there.

What's kept us here for 11 days — the length of our stay at *Playa Perla* — is the lure of emptiness. In this landscape — readymade with the sun, the moon, the stars, the wind, the birds, the sea, the shore critters, the rocks, the sand, and the cactus men standing, a chorus, at the back — we experience every minute detail in sharp focus, without interference or competition.

Some might see our sojourn as living on the edge of boredom, as in "Whatever shall we do today?" But the empty hours and empty spaces allow time for the precious reflections that don't arrive on an ordinary day. Here, the days pass, and we have noticed things we do not usually pay attention to. Our imaginations have migrated into new countries.

The days at *Perla,* for me, evolve into a form of meditation. I learn to love my flimsy gazebo, which protects me from the midday sun, the wind, the cold and prying eyes. I never spend a night when I don't wish for my thick box-springs back home, but I do not wish myself back in an inn in the towns, where the moon, the sun, and the coyotes we sometimes hear crying in the night, are too far away.

After one particular, bracingly cold swim, when the water feels pure and satiny, and I am doing my sissy sidestroke with another curious pelican floating on the surface a few feet away, I write in my journal — because I don't want to forget such a lucky state — "I feel fresher than I can ever remember!"

Between swimming and the hunger pains of dinner, Sandy and I lean back against the palm leaves of our *palapa* while I read *Harry Potter and the Sorcerer's Stone.* These huddles lead me to consider what part haphazardry has played in our arrival at this stark stretch, this place where *nada* rules, except the primary forces of nature and the human heart. I wonder if other turns in the rutted path would have led us to so rich a vacant amphitheater?

On the day that we pack up, Pablo comes by, hugs Sandy and Dorcy, and I suppose because I am the Matriarch, solemnly shakes hands with me. Eyes on the edge of tears, he vigorously assures us that, if we come back again next winter, he will not allow us to pay for our *palapas*. We will be *la familia*.

He will bring us scallops and clams daily. We will be his guests on *Playa Perla* — where the sea meets the shore, forming an almost-closing circle as he and the Great *cardon* watch over us.

Nepal: near Jharkot, 11,800 feet, peaks of Mustang in the far distance.

Postscript

Looking back over two decades, these words by Albert Camus, only recently discovered, reflect, exactly, my thoughts:

> *What gives value to travel . . . is the fact that, at a certain moment, when we are far from our own country . . . we are seized by a vague fear, and the instinctive desire to go back to the protection of old habits. This is the most obvious benefit of travel. At that moment, we are feverish, but also porous, so that the slightest touch makes us quiver to the depths of our being . . . we should not say that we travel for pleasure . . . It is an occasion for spiritual testing.*

The tracings of my compulsive explorations are clear.

I did not set out to test myself, but that IS what I did. My yearly exodus became "my work." Planning for it took over my mind and my muscles. Each time I instinctively reached for fresh horizons, raising the bar on the hurdles I set up for myself to conquer. Though I engaged in other activities between 1977 and 1999, the impressions gathered on these journeys are the truest autobiography of these decades.

I did not ever see myself as craving transformation, but Metamorphosis crept into my backpack — the inevitable sidekick, I now know, for one who strides out with a 'porous' heart.

Even if the tiniest alterations fall as light as rain, the psyche will eventually discover it has been deviously rearranged . . . dented . . . cracked . . . so that it delivers unexpected responses. The wayward sheep has, after all, strayed past the security of the fold and, whether it straggles back despairingly or triumphant, it won't be the same.

That was a different creature — the one who hovered drowsily under the protective arch of the doorway, reluctant to venture forth over the uneven potholes and push through the unlatched gate at the end of the pasture.

Lamb in the doorway, Hebrides.

At Callanish,1979.

About the Author

After 25 years in the role of suburban housewife and mother, Virginia Barton Brownback went back to college and launched a professional career in Language Arts and Photography. She taught at the Junior College level, traveled far afield, and exhibited her photography widely. She published her first story, a travel feature for the *Los Angeles Times*, when she was 62. After that, she worked regularly on contract for *Modern Maturity*, the AARP magazine. Since 1980, she has lived in Inverness, California, north of San Francisco, in a tight-knit community of shorebirds and environmental activists.